Praise for 'The Indisputable Gift of Men'

"I am hooked on this book! I was in meetings and running errands and couldn't wait to get back to the stories, and the men! Danna stimulated my mind, heart, and body as she passionately shared some of the most vulnerable moments in her life. While there were fabulous steamy sections there were also deeply heartfelt moments of massive growth and sweet moments of undeniable sadness. Thank you, Danna, for being the very needed and beautiful voice in a world desiring more for each and every one of us." Christine McIver, Founder of Inspired Choices Network

"The book reads well and I think the most intriguing thing about it is the refreshing honesty. I liked all the chapters about equally and think they are all pretty strong. I am very impressed by the quality and particular style of Danna's writing. It is very clean and very well crafted. She definitely has a gift and I am delighted she is pursuing it. One other thing I really liked is her serene attitude and avoidance of any male-bashing." Tom, AKA "Chapter 10"

"Knowing Danna has been a true gift, and one that has moved from one type of relationship to another in a seamless manner. When I revisited our time together through her writing I was astonished at her vivid recollection, her ability to transmit it in a clear manner, and the insight that she brought to the time we spent together." Matt, AKA "Chapter 8"

"You 'be' an awareness of a gift that men 'be.' You writing this book is actually inviting that information into the world. For me, coming out of a violent situation takes a lot of courage to put my foot in that water again and be in a relationship again. This book is creating a bomb of possibilities. How many people don't get the gift that men be? Don't know it's possible? And how many men don't know what a magnificent gift they are because they've chosen women that don't get it? I'm so grateful you wrote this book." Grace Hart, Author of *Beyond Domestic Violence*

"From the first chapter, I was hooked and couldn't put the book down. I knew it was something special when I found myself talking to the book and asking questions about what happened and why?! It was incredibly honest, sincere, and heart-touching. I found myself relating on many levels and starting to see my own dating in a new and refreshed way. I am buying several copies and gifting them to my friends. I believe we all need entertainment through education. Questioning the dating paradigm and their patterns is something I can see all single women needing to explore and evolve in choosing the 'right' partner in their lives. Thank you Danna for your incredible gift and perspective. I will forever be changed." Stephanie Beeby, Spiritual Business Coach and Founder of InFlowCEO.com, Hawaii

"This book captures a fantastic energy of connection, adventure, aliveness, and the joy of choice and receiving! As the mother of an eleven-year-old daughter, I believe the most empowering thing I can contribute to her having her own beautiful, healthy intimate relationships with men in the future is to teach her what this book embodies. I appreciate and celebrate Danna's invitation to honor the men in our lives by acknowledging what we have received from them. For me, her stories were like a surprise visit from a dear friend (all your best friends together in one friend). It was like free-falling into every delicious moment and being in a dance with the Universe. It drew me in and entangled itself in the most delightful way with beautiful memories of the men in my own life." Donna Hildebrand, Body Image and Relationship Coach, Mother, Wife, Speaker, and Author, Texas

"In this intimate, passionate, and courageous book, sensitive and highly intuitive coach Danna Lewis takes us on the well-travelled discovery of self and love. Through the search of a lifelong romantic partner, the journey forces us to break through the preconceived stereotypes of gender roles and differences. Danna shows us that gratitude is the way to conscious living. *The Indisputable*

Gift of Men is definitely a book written to empower women on their journey to new possibilities and abundance. Men, beware: you may too easily fall in love with Danna Lewis!" Jean-Michel Tournier, Former Rocket Scientist turned Linked In Digital Marketing Expert

The Indisputable Gift
of Men

Juli,

May you unwrap unexpected
& exquisite gifts.

xo, Danna

DANNA LEWIS

Printed in the United States of America

First Printing, 2019

ISBN-13: 978-1-949003-99-4 print edition
ISBN-13: 978-0-9627145-4-2 ebook edition

Published by DreamSculpt Books and Media
An imprint of Waterside Productions
2055 Oxford Ave
Cardiff, CA 92007
www.dreamsculpt.com
www.waterside.com

"You have given me a gift of finding in this life."
~Franz Kafka

Dedications

To the men in this book: I thank you for cherishing my heart, feeding my soul, adoring my body, nurturing my spirit, and inspiring my actions.

To Dr. Dain Heer and Gary Douglas: Thank you for empowering me to know what I know and for the gift of an ever-expanding consciousness in my life and in the world.

To my stepfather: Thank you for loving mom with such kindness and clear-heartedness and loving us like your own!

To my brothers: Thank you for being the husbands, fathers, and brothers you are! I love and am inspired watching you create your lives.

To women: You have the vulnerability, softness, sincerity, and strength to empower yourself, embrace the men in your life for the gifts they can be, and use your words to change this conversation.

To men: May you feel embraced and appreciated. May you be invited to go within and discover who you truly are, and what being a man, a gentleman, is for you.

Special Acknowledgements

To my personal book club and 'go-to' gals: thank you for your friendship, cheerleading, and practical wisdom for this project.

To Curry Glassell: thank you for your philanthropy, mentorship, and joy for this project. It truly got the book across the finish line!

To DreamSculpt: thank you for your excitement and belief in this book.

To Waterside Productions: thank you for your support and knowledge in getting the book to final publication!

To my first readers and reviewers: thank you for your feedback, enthusiasm, and the privilege of your time.

To my graphic designer, Lindy Chaffin-Start: thank you for your creativity and magic in collaborating with me on this beautiful book cover.

To my line editor, Joyce Walker: thank you for your talent and magic in finding the flaws and polishing this book into the gem it truly is.

To my photographer, Irina Bourova: thank you for always making it so easy and magical to create the most beautiful images together.

And, to Access Consciousness: thank you for the tools, facilitation, and hands-on healing techniques that have allowed past traumas and the energies that had manifested into PTSD to dissipate and nurture some of my greatest possibilities … so far.

Giving Forward

A portion of the proceeds from each book sale will be donated to the <u>National Domestic Violence Hotline (The Hotline)</u>.

The Hotline answers the call to support and shift power back to people affected by relationship abuse, they envision a world where all relationships are positive, healthy, and free from violence. 1 in 4 women and 1 in 7 men have experienced severe physical violence from an intimate partner in their lifetime. As the first point of contact for many affected by relationship abuse, The Hotline gives voice to the voiceless and have answered more than 5 million calls, digital chats and texts from people all over the US seeking support. If you or someone you know is affected by domestic violence contact www.thehotline.org. They offer services free of charge 24/7. *The contents of this book have not been endorsed by The Hotline.*

My wish is for men and women to heal their traumas and wounds, become empowered individuals, and begin to create the thriving, nurturing romantic partnerships that are truly possible.— Danna

The Indisputable Gift of Men

Table of Contents

"I don't want to get to the end of my life and find that I lived just the length of it. I want to have lived the width of it as well."
~Diane Ackerman

Chapter 1
The Invitation

It was two a.m. in the middle of my cozy terra-cotta-colored living room, music softly swirling through the air, with candlelight dancing between the shadows. Me? I was sitting cross-legged on the floor, having a slumber party with the Universe. We were strolling down memory lane, reminiscing about some pretty big changes.

Less than ten months earlier, I was standing in the middle of a very different living room 3,000 miles away with the sounds of packing tape running across the tops of boxes and a hornet's nest of emotions buzzing through the air. I was days away from leaving my life as a wife and vice president of a Fortune 50 company. And from leaving family and friends for the promise of following my heart to a place I had left it many years earlier.

While I had never lived in San Francisco, I had spent many summers, spring breaks, and winter holidays there when I was a teenager. My oldest brother, ten years my senior, arrived in the Bay Area right after leaving the army. My mother sent my second-oldest brother and me out to Marin many times to live with our big brother during school vacations. Looking back and wondering what she was thinking, I've never actually asked her, I'm grateful she gifted us those trips and very grateful she gifted herself the space to be a woman beyond being a single, hard-working mom.

Originally, my mom was not thrilled about my cross-country move. Her disapproval came partly from maternal instinct to want me near and partly from personal fear derived from her points of view of the world and how I should be engaging with it. While I may not have gotten my risk-taking, the-Universe-has-my-back positivity from her, I did get a soul-deep strength and tenacity that, all together, not only moved me across the country but also contributed to her and my stepfather impressively embracing the adventure and moving a few hours outside of San Francisco about six months after I did. I'm pretty sure my stepfather would do just about anything for my mom; I've always loved that about him. That he could be this space of so much ease, gentleness, and clear-hearted love for her. When they met, I was 11, my brother was 13, my stepfather's son was 12, and his daughter was maybe 7 who lived with her mother. Not only did he already have a sprouting teenager, but he was also willing to add two more to the mix! If that doesn't say, "true love," I don't know what does!

Children Were in That House
After a first marriage of turmoil, violence, and rage, it was pure relief and gratitude to move into a home of

peace. Well, except for all the teenage trauma and drama. Normal (ahhh, big sigh), n o r m a l teenage moodiness and madness! However, my preteen years, the first 11 years, were spent living with my biological father whose reaction to something as simple as dishes in the sink very likely could have been screaming anger, a rage of dishes being broken, or a fury of physical violence inflicted against my mother for any interpreted wrongness she or one of his children may have created.

My leftover seeds of post-traumatic stress come from growing up during a child's most impressionable years in a house that was more a war zone than a nurturing nest. The standards of perfection that could never be met and were always changing resulted, at any moment, in fits of anger, rage, and violence. Going to sleep at night, regardless of bedtime stories and snuggles, could mean being awakened to the sounds of screaming and hitting sometimes followed by our mother leaving to seek the safety of a domestic violence shelter for the night. Waking up in the morning, as much as I can recall, wasn't about the joy of a new day; it was about avoiding and side-stepping the unknown thing that would provoke an outburst of fury. To say it was terrifying is an understatement. It was, as all too many people know—domestic violence impacts one in four women and one in seven men—a constant state of fight or flight. Whether we acknowledge it or not, there really is an enormous amount of energy and emotion that gets wrapped around the axle of our life when we are in perpetual crisis mode. I just picture one of those older-model vacuums with all the debris and hair that gets wrapped around the bristly roller thing requiring so much more energy from you to push it forward while clogging it up and leaving it a bit impotent for doing its job.

Sometimes it was about me being the fierce voice of reason (at five!) and pleading for the peace and joy that childhood craves. Other times it was about me taking the courageous action of dialing 9-1-1 (at seven!) to literally save a life. I couldn't tell you if I did this once, twice, or a dozen times. Some details are blurred, others crystal clear. You see stories on the news of kids dialing 9-1-1 to save a parent who is hurt, perhaps has fallen down a flight of stairs, but to think that same child witnessed another person inflict that pain and that person was their other parent is almost incomprehensible. I've heard the saying that there is no greater pain than a parent losing a child to death. I say there is an almost irreparable pain in witnessing one parent physically harm the other.

While undeniably damaging, children, at least some children, seem to have a special strength that keeps their magic alive. While it may get buried in the pain, buried can be uncovered. So, for me, my pain was buried, along with my magic, to preserve the hope for a different future. And that future had delivered me to my first summer living in San Francisco after a fall and winter season of dating and mating. I couldn't resist, I did have fun being newly single and new to this spectacularly charming city.

A Home for a New Future

My charming city had provided the most charming ambiance for a handful of very charming men to sweep me off my feet with the most exquisite gifts I have ever received. So, after a day of strolling the sweeping hills of my Noe Valley neighborhood reminiscing about the magic that these men had brought into my life and wondering what the bleep it was all about, I found myself at two a.m. in the middle of my cozy terra cotta-colored living room, music softly swirling through the air with candlelight dancing between the shadows, sitting cross-legged on the floor, having a slumber party with the Universe.

"Truth," I said to the Universe, "what's the purpose of bringing these men into my life only to have them not be *the one*?" "Dare," said the Universe, "what do you know about the gifts of men that makes you *the one*?" And then it came…the words and stories in this book that tell the fairy tales of a future where men are not emasculated and women are empowered.

It came through my pores as a deep reflection, reconsideration, and finally, a receiving from men in a way that I hadn't known before. My home life, my experience as a child of domestic violence could have left me scared of men—as a toddler I would stand behind my mom's legs anytime a man approached. It could have left me scared of life and shut out and shut down from relationships. And while the pages have been steeping on the shelf, the "#MeToo" movement boiled the waters to a new roiling high of disparity between men and women.

From Jed Diamond, the Founder of The Good Men Project, "the era of powerful men and women who ignore sexual violence as simply 'men doing what men do' is over. In fact, it ended a hundred years ago when thousands of women, with the support of hundreds of men, fought for and passed the 19th amendment to the U.S. Constitution giving women the right to vote. It has continued with the *#MeToo movement,* which has broken the silence of sexual abuse forever" (*Jed Diamond, PhD, 12 Rules for Good Men, 1st edition, Waterside Productions 2019*).

The movement began to spread virally in October 2017 as a hashtag on social media in an attempt to demonstrate the widespread prevalence of sexual assault and harassment, especially in the workplace. I agree with social awareness, I agree with personal justice; my disagreement comes from the medicinal side effects that have pervaded our other sex, our men, into a misanthropic gender. Combine this with our current third wave of feminism as a reaction to earlier perceived failures of equality, and all poison-tipped arrows point directly to men as the enemy.

While anyone would understand if my past propelled me in the direction of being a feminist man-hater, ready to go to war with my fellow females, I have a different compass. One that points to my true north, around the battle, to a possibility of peace, a convergence of collaboration and communion, without discounting anyone else's personal story of trauma or diminishing any offense.

Where the Compass Leads, the Dance of Truth Follows

My compass lands me smack in the middle of an invitation that shines a light on the gift that men can be. And, more specifically, how a woman's romantic experience with men can transcend the expedition of dating to find *the one* into a journey of gratitude and receiving. The powers of gratitude and of receiving are oftentimes lost in the tunnel vision of goal attainment. The powers of gratitude and receiving have also been overshadowed by today's environment of expectations of what men are supposed to be. The comedian Kumail Nanjiani on *The Ellen DeGeneres Show* shared that, "the only emotion that men feel comfortable expressing, in general, is anger. We've been told that's the only manly emotion there is. Sadness isn't manly, fear isn't considered manly, even joy can be turned into anger. And I felt for many, many years I wasn't in touch with those emotions. I only felt comfortable showing anger." Much of society tells boys to be brave, to be physically powerful and reticent. Those boys grow up to be men, confused with their own emotions, often torn between traditional masculinity and their needs and desires to express themselves, to be nurturing, to share their deepest emotions.

The gender equality revolution hasn't allowed men to change alongside women. As women gained greater power and more opportunity, men started to lose the things they were taught made them "real men." Being a breadwinner wasn't guaranteed. As women began to show up in places where men had exclusively dominated—boardrooms, the armed forces, Congress—men who had once felt safe to talk as they please were now somewhat imprisoned by a culture of political correctness. Neither right nor wrong, but strategic awareness of what is occurring, the cultural shift has left some confused, others feeling powerless, and a lot of men angry.

The powers of gratitude and receiving have no room to exist in this space of judgment.

Herb Goldberg, author of *The Hazards of Being Male,* commented that "the male has paid a heavy price for his masculine 'privilege' and power. He is out of touch with his emotions and his body. He is playing by the rules of the male game plan and with lemming-like purpose, he is destroying himself– emotionally, psychologically, and physically" (Herb Goldberg, The Hazards of Being Male: Surviving the Myth of Masculine Privilege, 1st edition, Iconoclassics Publications, 2009).

Innately, men desire to provide. While I hesitate to relate this back to caveman days for obvious reasons, the physiology and physicality of men being stronger, being hunters, and being providers for women still trickle through their DNA. Women were distinctly more of the multitaskers, the gatherers, having diffuse awareness of their environment, their families, and their men. While women were cooking, feeding, sewing, and nurturing, men had one focus, one very important, vital focus: to hunt and, literally, provide. There are exceptions, there are outliers, and there are pissed-off women cursing me right now, calling me all sorts of names. That's okay. There are also many who perceive the lightness and truth to how this still floats in the spaces between the molecules. That men would like to show up with and for us, collaborate, create, and appreciate us in a way only they can.

They are not adversaries and not inherently trying to steal or keep anything from us. There are huge discrepancies in men choosing their innate gifts and those showing up in our traumatized times. There are also huge discrepancies with how women treat men, the gentlemen in the former, with respect, admiration, kindness, and gratitude. The sitcom landscape portrays men as incompetent, childlike, bumbling idiots. Sometimes they are portrayed as sweet, well-meaning idiots (i.e., Homer Simpson, Jack Duckworth, Tim from *The Office*); sometimes pig-headed, blundering idiots (i.e., the Mitchell brothers, Frank in *Shameless*, Larry David in *Curb Your Enthusiasm*); and sometimes they are sex-mad idiots (i.e., Charlie in *Two and a Half Men*, Joey in *Friends*).

And, in real life, many women talk about and treat men with stifling criticism, disrespect, and emasculation. You've seen it, you've heard it, and perhaps you've participated in it or initiated it. Many of us have. And, without shame, blame, regret, or guilt, I ask you to read on.

In my journey, the experiences that have contributed most dynamically to me have been my experiences with the men I've dated. I chose to be in the moment of who they were (at the time) and who we were together instead of attempting to change them or us in any way. By shifting my perspective from a conclusion of "he's not the one" to a question of "what gift is he to me?" I shifted my life from one of feeling inhibited and lost to one of empowerment and appreciation for my own capacity to create my life, to be responsible for my happiness, and to choose relationship as a contribution in a way I had never done before and in a way I did not quite know that I could.

The book came from a profound desire to identify, acknowledge, and document the pure beauty of what had been offered to me. A beauty so intensified from its organic vulnerability, it illuminated me from within. And then it sat. It sat quietly over the years, every so often tugging at me, reminding me of its existence.

Sometimes I would catch a glimpse of the illuminated beauty filtering out from its pages in the corner of my mind. I wondered and called myself to task to figure out if this book could be a contribution to the world. The reaction of my early readers was always the same—tears and laughter of deep connection to the stories and the simplicity of universal truth in them. They were inspired to recall, review, and revere in what they may have been unwilling to know, be, perceive, receive from their own stories with men. And, they expressed deep gratitude for the space that was created for them to do so.

My hope, my pleading hope and insatiable desire, is for this book to ignite a revolution of grace. Grace in discovering and acknowledging the gifts you've received; praise for yourself in digging deep to let go, forgive, and find those gifts; and gratitude (fingers crossed) extended outward so that the men may know the gifts they provided. I ask for a world where women choose to empower themselves in dating, in partnership, and in life. A world where we strive to learn more about the other sex and understand each other not with tolerance, but with allowance. A world where we have cultivated our own confidence and connectedness within ourselves that nurtures us into receiving (with kindness and gratitude) the gift that men truly can be in our lives.

With Joy & Gratitude, XO, Danna

★　*Do you desire space to reflect and journal? Visit the "Invitation to Go Deeper" section at the end of the book.*

"What if every experience is an invitation to something greater … an empowerment of you?"
~Danna Lewis

Chapter 2
The RSVP: The Gift of Presence

I had the pleasure of having a traditional Passover Seder this year at my brother's house in San Rafael, California. It was a motley crew of my extended family— my brother (who is actually my half-brother), his five-year-old triplets (my niece and two nephews), his girlfriend, her eight-year-old son, her 17-year-old daughter, my brother's mother, my brother's stepfather, and my brother's aunt (his mother's sister). Did you get all that? A nice, traditional mishmash of a family. Some not Jewish, most not very religious unless there's food involved, and a few older, wiser, and more religiously educated than the rest.

The table was moved into the living room so that we could insert the two extra leaves to accommodate the dinner for 11. It was beautifully set with china, linens (a tablecloth and cloth napkins), candles, crystal wine glasses, and the silver service. All meticulously presided over by the strict supervision of my brother's mother who, along with her husband, used to own and run a four-star French restaurant near Santa Cruz, California. I think it took three of us to set the table while my brother's stepfather and mother prepared the traditional Passover Seder feast. You just don't miss a meal when these two are cooking. My mouth is watering just thinking about the food. We were lucky to have my brother's aunt in attendance as well to preside over the "teaching" and navigate us through each step of the traditional supper.

Ghosts of Now

Part of the tradition of the Passover Seder is to leave the front door of the house open so that the ghost of Elijah the prophet can enter the home. As a servant of God and a man of prayer, Elijah is a good ghost, and this is a good thing to invite him into your home. Although I always thought that ghosts could pretty much pass through doors and walls and other such phenomenon, so that kind of challenges the whole leaving the door open thing except that it is more polite and welcoming. I'm all about being polite, and with three kids living in the house, the door being open was a given.

So, as we sat around the Passover table eating, drinking wine (we had poured the Manischewitz out—tradition absolutely went down the drain, along with the bad wine—in favor of a 90-point red cabernet), enjoying the pace and involvement of the traditional Seder, my sister-in-law announced that she "felt" the presence of Elijah.

My five-year-old niece promptly replied, "There are presents, I don't see them, where are the presents?!"

From the mouths of babes, a true five-year-old: always entertaining and always enlightening.

I reflect on that moment with the delighted joy of accepting the invitation to attend such a memorable evening, and with satisfied joy in knowing that I have finally allowed myself to be aware of my "presence" so that I can find the "presents" in every situation.

My Invitation to You

I invite you to reflect on and review the present. What invitations literal and otherwise have you perhaps missed or ignored? I wonder if you would be present with them, if there is actually something there that you have been asking for? Things don't always show up the way you think they will; that invite to your nephew's baseball game may lead you right to your lifelong partner or new best friend or business opportunity. Be willing to check in with yourself and trust the whisper of awareness that is lighting your path to the something greater that you have been asking for.

As I sit writing today, I could have chosen to do so from the cozy comfort of my sofa on this foggy, cold San Francisco summer morning. However, I choose to follow the whisper of awareness that had me walk 1½ miles uphill (and I mean UP hill, the Fillmore hill to Pacific Heights for those of you that know San Francisco) carrying my computer and work stuff, bundled up and panting. Sure, for the big, big chocolate chip cookie at The Grove, that's my easy answer. But really, it was for the whisper of awareness that tickled my ear on this

Monday morning to choose something different among all the places; choose something different and end up sitting next to a fellow writer. End up sitting next to fellow possibilities yet to be explored.

> *I admire, applaud, and appreciate your courage,*
> *XO, Danna*

★ *Do you desire space to reflect and journal? Visit the "Invitation to Go Deeper" section at the end of the book.*

"It's the possibility that keeps me going, not the guarantee."

~Nicholas Sparks

Chapter 3

The Empty Box: the Gift of Possibility

*M*ost gifts are thoughtfully chosen, delicately wrapped, and presented with anticipation and joy. I'm sure if someone handed you an empty box and said, "Here, I saw this and thought of you." you would be baffled, maybe even irritated, and quite possibly ungrateful. But a true gift satisfies a want or need that you might not have even been aware of. In this story, my story, the empty box represents me in 2005-2006. My heart, my soul, and my spirit were all empty except for the air of hope. My "Eat, Pray, Love" moment of when I had everything, and yet nothing seemed to feel right. A marriage to a good man, a successful career, wonderful friends, a loving family, and a beautiful home. But I was void of light and energy and in its place, despair, heartache, ambivalence, bitterness, guilt, and shame. Why was I void? I hear my coach's voice in my head. That's the million-dollar question and priceless answer. It was a malaise on steroids not created by wrong choices, but simply created by life choices now awakening into awareness like a sleeping giant coming out of hibernation. My life was demanding something different than the life I thought I was supposed to have. Raise your hand if you've rubbed that sleep from your eyes, if you've fallen out of the bed of someone else's life, bewilderingly wondering what else is possible.

The Inconceivable Fur Baby Love

My dog, Harley, my child and fur baby in this lifetime, had lost his will after 14 months of illness. After 11 happy, healthy, boisterous years, he just collapsed one night while walking down the long hallway toward me. I freaked out in a surreal crisis intervention, there's no way this is happening, race to the emergency room way! He was put on life support—literally—put into a medically induced coma and on breathing machines so the vets could figure out what the heck was going on and then allow the treatment to begin to work. It was a blur with sparks of colors; the colors of my credit cards as I grabbed them out of my wallet and tossed them to the receptionist for the quickly mounting bill. When your little heart of feisty, protective, snuggledom is fighting for his life, there's no limit to what you will pay.

After doing a multitude of tests and eliminating the most common possible causes, twenty-four hours later he was diagnosed with a very rare case of meningitis and given a 50 percent chance of survival. And so I handed over another credit card and my frantic soul to the animal hospital team. This was a little dog weighing maybe

12 pounds with 12 tons of gusto for life—he was going to live. We, my husband at the time and I, were there as much as possible during the week he spent in the hospital (about three days in ICU and then the rest of the time recovering) until the point we were able to take him home. Family and friends called nonstop to check on him; there was so much love and concern. I can still recall the outpouring of love as if it were yesterday.

He did come home about a week later. He was so weak from the disease, medicines, and lack of movement that he was unable to stand on his own for a bit. We had to carry him outside and hold him up to go potty. Oh my gosh, my heart is hurting just writing this. Not just from what was going on with his body, but from the unconditional love we had for him and the complete commitment to his care. It turned out my sweet boy was as sensitive to medicines as I am; he was afflicted with every medicinal side effect possible from the cocktail of drugs he was given. The prednisone that saved his life also gave him diabetes. Me, the girl who fainted at her own medical procedures and sight of needles, was now getting her dog to pee in a cup (little paper Dixie cups!), checking blood sugar levels, and administering insulin shots! It was a roller coaster of emotions. It was celebrations when he beat the odds, regained his strength, met life with his old fervor, and it was fear and tenacity when another ailment struck: lesions from antibiotics, a pancreatitis attack, cataracts from the diabetes. But the boy was a fighter, and his quality of life was, oddly, barely compromised. When the cataracts showed up, I cried and cried, wondering how he was going to get around, and I cried even more because he wouldn't be able to see me anymore, his pup mama. But Harley, he barely missed a step, other than us making sure not to move the furniture around, Harley was trotting along within days, still chasing after ducks and still running with confidence!

It Takes a Village

That dog's last year was filled with more love, devotion, and attention than many children receive their entire lives. Our entire family showed up to help us with his care. Because the diabetes required a midday blood sugar check, we devised a schedule where different family members could either have him for the day or come to the house to check on him. I'm still in awe of this. Each time I pulled into the driveway on my designated day to run home from work during lunchtime, I would hold my breath ... and pray ... that my boy was still alive for another day. One day a week, I drove him across town in the morning to stay with my parents for the day. My in-laws and husband were all very much involved with the schedule as well, all taking turns to check on our little pup. And, as I write this, I'm now amused at the times I've thought a parent's obsessive attention and scheduling of their children was overboard! Lest we forget our own intensity and insanity where love is concerned. Wink, wink.

And then the day did finally come when his body began shutting down. Letting go was the choice we had to make. He looked at me and made a sigh he had never uttered before. He rolled over so I could rub his belly. I looked into his eyes, and I just knew. I was his pup mom. I actually had always known every ache and pain, every enjoyment. And, looking back, what I haven't mentioned yet is that I knew something was wrong weeks before he collapsed in the hallway. I walked by him one evening, and I had a whisper of awareness that something wasn't right. My husband waved it off. And without any outward signs from Harley, so did I. This time, in absolute knowing, I knew it was time to let his little body go and his spirit be free. I was in complete peace with my choice. It was actually the first choice I had ever made that I felt so utterly right and peaceful about.

During these same 14 months of navigating Harley's health, I was also attending a full load of evening university courses, managing my team at work, having a house built, and getting by but not getting along with my husband. While I was thinking long-term of my career, moving to California eventually, and possibly having children, we were in agreement with that bigger picture. We were not, however, in agreement with the daily living taking place. His career and life goals didn't match my level of ambition or desire, and I found myself leaning into my masculine energy to create and collaborate with him, resulting in increasing criticism and emasculation of him. My femininity was frustrated and feverishly needing to be comforted and cared for. I'm not quite sure how I actually made it through each day. Do you have those memories and recollections of situations so intensely stressful and demanding that afterward you're in shock and perhaps a bit in awe that you actually did get through it? Oh my gosh, I remember my hair falling out from the stress, anxiety attacks, the exhaustion, and the little bit of comfort I received in prayer, listening to contemporary Christian music, and in knowing I was not alone, that the Universe somehow had my back. Yes, Christian music. Yes, me the 'Jewish girl' finding comfort and peace in Christian music.

We always hear and tell others in crisis that God/the Universe does not give us anything we cannot handle. Have you ever called "Bullshit" on that? I certainly have! But I also hang on to every word in that saying, like I hung on to every breath that Harley took on his own when we removed the breathing tube from his throat. A cough. A catch. A gulp. And finally, a breath. A breath to another step forward into life.

But now I knew I had to be the one to take that same breath away from him for his spirit to move into peaceful doggy heaven. I'm quite sure it exists; how could such providers of unconditional love and joy not have a heaven? I truly experienced God that day as I held Harley in my arms, under a tree outside of the animal hospital, while the doctor gave him the silent injection. There is no other way to explain the strength it took to hold him in my arms and let his body die so his spirit could be free again.

There are very few places where we are bestowed the responsibility of literally choosing life, to end a life. Abortion rights, women having the right to choose what is best for their body, is an unending debate as it takes into account another's life. Having a sick child or sick parent and being the legal custodian of directing healthcare with the ultimate choice of ending that life when the conditions present themselves is unimaginable to most and intimately known to too many.

Owning a pet and owning the exclusive rights of choosing their healthcare to me is also an omnipotent responsibility that I did not take lightly. While the knowledge of when it was time actually had intense ease, picking him up and carrying him out of the house for the last time was intensely surreal. I think time stopped. Reality stopped. I just did and moved, not like a robot without feeling, more like a warrior on a mission to bring peace back to a being whose body was no longer his home but enemy territory filled with disease.

And I moved as a stealth warrior that day, scooping Harley up in my arms, holding him in my lap in the car without any worry of having to put on his doggy seatbelt, carrying him into the veterinarian hospital to a sea of faces that had come to know and love him endearingly. The day unfolded simultaneously in slow motion and fast forward; time is not real in matters of life, love, and death. As the energy crossed universal boundaries and we finally did get to that moment under the tree where his body was no longer his body, "time of death" became but a singular moment in the construct known as time. Harley, however, became the infinite being in the boundless space between the molecules once again.

So, when I'm asked how I felt about it, I'm not sure I was feeling. I was actually being with the full commitment that was required of me, what I agreed to when he came into my life. And really, there is no word in English, that I've discovered, to succinctly express being a stealth warrior facilitating a being out of its earth body to universal consciousness.

The Unrecognizable Life

And once he was gone, the shock and grieving began. I sobbed so, so much. Years later, I now know that the intense feelings of loss are so much related to the physicality of our relationship, to the loss of not having his physical body with me, as we are always connected through our beings. I loved my grandmother and all my grandparents, but when they died, although I was sad, I did not experience intense grieving or loss. They weren't a part of my daily life; I was rarely in their physical presence. But, holy cow, the physical pain that comes from a physical loss is excruciating and shocking. That shock did insert me squarely into living in the present. His death propelled me into my existing life of school to finish, the house construction project to navigate, work to perform, and a failing marriage to confront. I would say that I handled it the only way I could at the time ... with a nervous breakdown.

My anxiety and panic attacks were constant waves hitting the shore of my spirit. I was on a constant dose of antianxiety medication and sleeping pills. I was so exhausted and felt so unhealthy. I could not even look at myself in the mirror. The devastation and despair were so great, I was at a complete loss as to how to live and had to remind myself to breathe. I can't count the number of times at work when I would go to the nurse's office to sit in a corner, breathe into a paper bag, and try to disappear from life, my present-day existence. I just couldn't bear the pain. Looking back, I realize I was in that precious space of moving from being strangely comfortable with raw discomfort that had become my life to knowing that stepping forward into the unknown could not be worse.

People were just as much at a loss as to how to help me. But they offered sympathy and encouragement. They gave me permission to just be. "Go breathe into a paper bag if you need to, nobody is judging you," I remember one of my coworkers telling me. Until this point in my life, I had been a more private person, especially at work. But my pain was so obvious, talking about it was the only way through it. And my body and heart soaked up the attention and support. My friend Lynne would stop by my desk and just leave bags of fat-filled organic granola because she knew I was only eating a few bites a day. We began joking about filling the candy dish with Xanax. People were sharing their own stories. I was listening and receiving. It was incredibly helpful and healing.

Finally, the house building process was complete. My husband and I moved into our new house, and I started to unpack. I thought that as I unpacked, I was physically settling into the next phase of my life, physically moving forward into a new, happier place with my husband by physically moving into our new home. I really was excited about having built and participated in designing our home from the ground up. It was in a neighborhood that provided the walkability, the village feel that I have always loved so much. All the obsessive and incessant decorating that had been going on in my head now had an outlet! My energy had a direction filled with swatches, colors, and measuring tapes. Let the projects begin! I've always had the capacity to walk into a room and have an almost instantaneous vision of function and beauty for it. Having the blank canvas of decorating a new house was pure creative heaven for me. The truism here is that while you can decorate and beautify, you cannot ignore the structural inefficiencies, because they always find a way of showing through.

So six weeks later, I moved out of the new house and in with my second family: my friend, her husband, and two kids. The new house with the new furniture in the new neighborhood did not give me new happiness, so I moved out, across town to something familiar.

My second family, so warm, welcoming, and comforting. My poor husband had no idea what to do except pray and wait and beg me to go to marriage counseling. We had been to a few marriage counselors previously during our eight-year marriage with little to show for it. But I did go with him to the marriage counselor. This one was different. This one was blunt, forthright, and had a progressive approach. This time I was learning things that were helpful and productive; tools for a healthy relationship. Although unsure, and looking back, probably more out of fear than love, six weeks later I moved back in with my husband ... to the new house, with new hope. My husband was devastated when I left. Loving me so much and hurting so much for my joy and adoring that was lost in the struggle to continue to create together from different points of view. And, now with me home again, I would say he was excited, scared, and cautiously optimistic.

I am sure a lot of you have been there, or maybe you are there now. I know how dark it is at the bottom of that empty box, dare I say "well of despair"? This "dark night of the soul" or spiritual crisis references the sort of spiritual crisis or detox that someone has to go through to "wake up" to a different possibility. But if you're experiencing it and don't know what's happening, it can be really intense and scary. Some signs that indicate a spiritual healing crisis include feeling you "should" be happy because technically you should but aren't (like me with my great husband and career and new house); an innate purging of things from your life in physical, emotional, and energetic ways; your need to be authentically you (and discovering what that is) overrides your need to impress anyone; and/or you feel like you are or could die. And something in you actually is dying; it's the beliefs and structures that no longer meet the desires of your genuine self.

Sometimes hope, or as I experienced in later years, a deep knowing, no matter how wispy or insignificant it may seem, is what holds us fast to taking another, no matter how tiny, step forward. I've had my share of the shock and initiation of spiritual crises over the years, and truly each has moved and sometimes hurled me forward into the beauty of who I am. I wish the same for you, the last part, the very last part, "…the beauty of who you are." The hurling, twirling, nauseating, dizzying ride of the dark night, uh, yeah, if any of us could skip that, hallelujah!

Unrecognizable Strength

So where am I today? In a place of inner peace. How do I know this? Because a few months ago, I was sitting in my new apartment in San Francisco with hardly any friends, no job, no titles (vice president of such and such, wife, homeowner, etc.) in the midst of the total chaos of building a new life, and I felt ... completely peaceful.

Some people have their identities stripped away. I chose to walk away from mine and deconstruct my life. I went from being married, living in a one-year-old house we had built, being close to lots of family and friends, and having a job as a vice president of operations at a Fortune 50 company to getting divorced, selling the house, resigning from my job, and moving across the country to California where I knew maybe a handful of people including my two brothers. I had no idea what effect that choice would create. I went through a period of not even knowing how to introduce myself to people. It seems like one of the first things we talk about with new people is our job and our spouses. After a while of stumbling through this, I finally just started introducing myself simply with my name. Sometimes I would add that I was on sabbatical, recharging, renewing, or recreating my life. That sounds so mysterious and charming. And if you let yourself go there, to that sometimes dark, scary place of standing with your arms outstretched saying, "I am me, who am I?" your life may show up to charm, mystify, and enchant you.

My Invitation to You

Let's open one of your empty boxes, together, and uncover the gift of possibility. Grab a cup of tea or cocoa or perhaps a glass of wine or a cocktail, turn off your phone. I promise the sky won't fall and whoever or whatever is needing you will survive the next few minutes without your instant reply ... really, it's all about you right now!

Take a deep breath and with Harrison-Ford-Indiana-Jones curiosity and courage, go back into the empty box of one of your dark nights. Stand in the middle of that total darkness, knowing you are safe and sound in the present. Stand in the middle of that total darkness and be still with it. Stand in the middle of that empty box that you had and ask yourself this: If I could suspend my belief that anything here was right or wrong; that I must defend for or against my story, the story, could there be a new possibility to light the way?

Barriers down, vulnerability up, was there an unacknowledged spiritual healing occurring? Beyond the surface decisions, thoughts, and meanings of a dark time, could it have actually been a spiritual healing experience that was required to restore harmony to your being? A deep learning created to consciously reconnect with your inner truth and wisdom?

Allow yourself to notice the clues lingering in the corners, longing for your attention. Was your dark night actually moments of change and transformation threaded together by your demand for something greater to show up in your life? Were the actions of purging, of drastic change, of intense pain and hurt the clearing of what was no longer serving you?

While it may not be staunchly evident in this moment, please allow the quantum entanglements of the Universe to continue to fill that empty box with sun-dappled illumination.

I admire, applaud, and appreciate your courage,
XO, Danna

---

* *Do you desire space to reflect and journal? Visit the "Invitation to Go Deeper" section at the end of the book.*

"We don't receive wisdom; we must discover it for ourselves after a journey that no one can take for us or spare us."
~Marcel Proust

Chapter 4

Transportation: The Gift of Perspective and Wisdom

Have you ever read *O!* magazine? Oprah interviews people about their "Aha!" moments, and I remember thinking to myself in my sometimes (often) dramatic way, "I'm a lost soul, I haven't had an "Aha!" moment, Oh My God, what's wrong with me, when will I have my "Aha!" moment?!" Anyone else have that or is it just me? Anyone? ANYONE?!

Well, I am going to share a story with you that was, and still is, the most valuable, life-changing lesson I have ever learned, PERIOD. And the thing is, it's so integral to authentic living, to spiritual savvy, and to traveling through life with and from the space of consciousness. Not unlike recycling is to our contribution to saving the planet and tree-hugging and barefoot walking is to grounding and being grounded to ourselves and the earth. Perspective is the transportation to higher ground, to the inclusion of everything without judgment. So here it is...are you ready...it is so simple...do I sound like an infomercial?...here we go...find the "gift" that lies in every situation, every experience, every person and you will find your spirit of compassion and allowance. And, you will empower yourself to continue to choose and create greater in your own life. You will move from that place of grievance, shame, and resentment to—you got it hippie girls—love, peace, and harmony. Go ahead, picture yourself sitting in a field of flowers with butterflies fluttering around you. I've been to that place. It's glorious.

Believe me, I am a reformed (and still working on it) perfectionist, complainer, and fault-finder. Harboring those low-frequency thoughts, feelings, and emotions creates, for lack of a better word, ickiness, sludge, drudge, and decay. Change your perspective, find the "gift," change your thoughts, and your feelings will follow. And, from the world of quantum physics, change the energy and the physical actualization of something different will be able to follow suit.

Let me explain further. Let's take my desire to have more ease and elegance in living. I clearly recall acknowledging, meditating, and doing "energy pull exercises" based on snippets of things I had seen or experienced that to me created more ease and elegance in living: having multiple options for exercise and movement in the apartment and outside; having the house cleaned without me having to make it happen; having healthy food options available at home along with some unexplainable things that truly were energies I had noticed and said, "oh, yes, that!" And then, a little while later, one day I was peddling on my exercise bike, listening to a personal development book on Audible, organic prepared, ready-to-make smoothies in the freezer when my housekeeper arrived to clean, and I gallantly smiled and said, "Yes, this!" to myself in an excited, slightly dubious exclamation of my creation. I had changed the energy of what was before frenetic inconsistency to bringing together something that worked really well for me. I know you may be thinking, "Well that's easy, you go online order an exercise bike, join a subscription food service and call a housecleaner." Yes, that is true; you can do that. But, you can't do that before you've shifted the energy into being able to receive those gifts. And, if you're like me, an energetic, empathic being, you require more than basic options. We require conscious possibilities.

When it came to shifting the energy currently occurring with my soon to be ex-husband and the money situation, how did I learn this magical life lesson of finding the gift? The hard way. Oh, the hard, pissed off way, of course. But, I learned it well.

Proud and Pissed Off

I was in the midst of my divorce, and regardless of how amicable it was, there were moments of discord, anger, and vengefulness. That's what happens when you mix emotions with legal matters; it's human nature. I walked into my divorce with the intention of being respectful, compassionate, and kind. My grace is extremely important to me. It didn't matter what anyone said, suggested, or implied that I do. And let me tell you, there were some not nice, downright bitchy, nasty things people suggested … out of the goodness of their hearts, of course. I was the one who I would be waking up with when it was all said and done. My self-righteous self wanted to wake up knowing that I maintained my grace and integrity without losing my sense of self or the shirt off my back. Although, as you'll find out later, being naked with the shirt off your back is a good thing, and naked in San Francisco is welcomed, accepted, and unnoticed.

This is a true testament to how people look at the same, exact situation and interpret it entirely differently. Which makes sense because if my ex-husband and I didn't perceive things so differently, maybe we wouldn't have been getting a divorce. This isn't rocket science. My viewpoint was I go through the house, decide who gets what, apply values to the possessions, then make it all fair and just with the cash flow. I did spend 17 years in Corporate America, mostly in financial services, so this seemed like a very natural thing to me. If I wanted an expensive piece of art or furniture, then I would receive less money from the cash funds or offset with other less expensive items. My ex-husband, for whatever reason(s), and I'm not going to begin to speak for him, did not have this same viewpoint. He felt that we go through the house, decide who gets/wants what, including the cars we were currently driving, and call it a day. He wasn't willing to address the value discrepancy of assets along with the cash flow.

Hmmmm. Well, I know that in a marriage, you are partners, and you are supposed to share things equally. I fell into the deep end of selfish bitterness and regret for having given up the cute, sexy convertible I had been driving so that he could have a brand-new truck as part of his business. For the greater good of the relationship, I had bought him the truck, and it now seemed very unfair as I sat in his old four-door sedan I was being left with. Let's just say I was livid. And I truly apologize to my ex-husband for sharing this possibly negatively perceived intimate story, but it is truly how I learned this vital lesson in my life. So, once again, for the greater good, I am sharing.

Did I mention that I was livid? For days I sat with this. Fuming. And yes, it occurred to me that it was just money, but I felt like it was my hard-earned money, and yes, I totally get my greed and selfishness in thinking that the money I earned during my marriage was "my" money. I am such a generous, altruistic person by nature, but I could not reconcile this situation in my mind. I'm admitting my own fault here, and I knew then I had to find a way to feel good about this no matter the financial impact or outcome of mediation. My life coach, (my motivating, supportive life coach Dianne) told me that there was a gift in this situation and I should find it. Ummm, sure, a gift. That would be me giving my ex a car that I paid for or maybe the gift of learning not to be so damn kind and generous. Okay, not what you were expecting to hear. Allow me to finish ...

Surrendering to the Surprise

During this time, I was reconnected with a very dear old friend of mine, Bob. Umm, actually friend / past lover / soul connection of many lifetimes to be super-clear.

Turned out, my realtor used him exclusively as his title agent. Small world. I hadn't seen him in years but had known him for about fifteen years and, through the sale of the house, got to see him again and learn that he had been diagnosed with Lou Gehrig's disease. It was heartbreaking for me to find out that someone I have known since we were about 22, a man who was always so vivacious, audacious, and pompous, was so ill.

I'm a researcher. I like to learn about things, especially if they touch my life in some way. So there I was, on the Internet, reading about Lou Gehrig's disease, and there *it* was: "Donate your car to help Lou Gehrig's research." Well, I didn't donate my car, but what I did do was decide, in that instant, to donate half of the proceeds of the sale of my car (I knew I would sell it before I moved to San Francisco) to my friend's healthcare fund.

Yes, it was a tangible gift but really, please, look deeper. We are given knowledge every day. Taking that knowledge and intentionally turning a toxic matter into a product of kindness and generosity, well, that is the gift of wisdom. And, instantaneously all of my bitterness and anger around the car situation with my ex dissipated. Poof, gone!

From that moment forward, I have actively looked for the gift in every situation. Because of this drastic change in perspective, there has been a drastic change in me.

My Invitation to You

Who's ready for a turning point in the road to the super-highway of consciousness? Just for you, I have a few fun tools to jumpstart you in shifting the gears on your perspective. Start asking the following questions when looking for the gift:

1. What's right about this I'm not getting?
2. What point of view would I have to shift, change, or give up for this to turn out greater than I can imagine?
3. When all else fails: "Universe, show me the gift here."

And, please, please, please invoke your some-times-impossible patience and do not rush, push, or plot for an answer. Discovering the gift is an unfolding, a soft whisper of awareness, a gentle release, and yes, sometimes a thunderous roar. Hmmm, like our sometimes elusive orgasms ladies, the awareness of the gift cannot be forced, it will come when it chooses to come!

I admire, applaud, and appreciate your courage,
XO, Danna

★ *Do you desire space to reflect and journal? Visit the "Invitation to Go Deeper" section at the end of the book.*

"You and I are essentially infinite choice-makers. In every moment of our existence, we are in that field of all possibilities where we have access to infinite choices."
~Deepak Chopra

Chapter 5

Shopping: The Gift of Intention and Choice

I am on my journey to find my love, which as I sit here writing, I have not found yet, but I can feel it just around the corner. Maybe around the corner from the Starbuck's two doors down from my apartment or maybe the other corner where the yummy gelato place is (my second home during times of heartache). I'm not sure which corner, but I know it's there. When I got married, I actually knew in a very subtle way that it wasn't my best choice, it wasn't backed with the confidence of knowing it was something that was true to the longevity of my life and living. It was, however, a huge contribution in many ways, including many moments of awareness from that one, big choice.

You know, "live and learn" and my personal philosophy, choice creates awareness. With marriage and relationship, being such a strong and significant structure in so much of society, I had not actually asked myself if it was true for me. If relationship and marriage were actually what I desired to have. I just wonder how many of you reading this have given yourself the space to explore this for yourself. Being single has been criticized and wronged for much of the Western world. You are born, you grow up, you go to school, you get married, you have kids (and the house and the dog and the promotions), and you ... you get the idea; it's instilled and insinuated into the infrastructure of our lives. I'll never forget how it showed up like an uninvited guest at the housewarming party my friends threw for me for my first house. My first house—that I bought—for myself.

I had recently moved back from New York City and was happy to be with old friends again and embarking on a new journey of homeownership. The party was winding down, people were leaving, everyone had been so excited to celebrate with me. And as my grandmother was walking out, literally with a kiss on the cheek and one foot out the door, she leaned back in and said, "Mazel tov, I love your new home, it would look better with a man it." Not kidding! We had taken bets, we had expected it, and yet when it landed, it still stung. And there you have it folks, through no fault of her own, our insistent structure in this society of coupling had inserted itself into my celebratory single-woman success.

P.S.

A few months later, I did add a man to that house, a man who became my husband. Because, for me, there is a power and pleasure in a romantic partnership that I absolutely embrace and adore. Having a person, "your person" to cuddle up with, play with, learn about and from, mmmmhmmm, I love this. I enjoy the nakedness of it literally and figuratively. I enjoy the patterns, rituals, intimacy, and dynamics that only exist with you and that person. I humbly recognize the choice we make of bearing witness to not only someone else's life in a wildly authentic and vulnerable way, but of the life you are creating together day-to-day.

I've been sexy and single, I've been sad and single, I've been sappy and coupled, I've been somber and coupled, and I've experienced so, so much before, during, and after all the spaces of my life defined by having a man next to me or not. What I have come to know through the kaleidoscope of living is that, for me, I will always choose partnership.

I choose the communion that comes from the big choice, the big, juicy commitment of romantic partnership. When it is done from the space of conscious leadership, from deep presence, interdependence, and engagement with one another to nurture, honor, and contribute to one another and the entity of the partnership you have entered. I choose the deliciousness of living with someone and with knowing someone in an unabashed, naked (in every sense of the word) way. I choose the awkward, wonky, going sideways moments that demand vulnerability and that, when chosen, open up the space for communion so beyond what societal norms of relationship have bastardized and so spectacularly exquisite the earth sighs with gratitude.

That's me. That's what I choose for me. And, if you were to truly look at this for yourself, which I sincerely hope that you do, what is true for you? If there was no right or wrong, good, perfect and correct choice, only the choice that could create the most for you, for what you desire and for what you require, what would you choose?

Your Turn
Look at it.

Really, truly look at it. For you and no one else's expectations or projections of you. If you could have it all your way, what would you choose?

Ahhhh, there you go. That. That energy, that thing you just landed on, at least for a moment, if not longer. It may be a cognitive set of ideas and descriptions, and it may be an energy that fluttered within you. All of that together is what I'm talking about. Please don't dismiss the flutter, the energy of something, just because you don't have words for it. The words can be figured out or not. You had it (the energy) and you knew it. Keep tapping into that energy, ladies, and now...let's go shopping!

The most pragmatic way to go shopping is with a list. And, if you're shopping for a lover, a boyfriend, a husband, or something in between, in the midst of your busy life, save yourself a whole lotta drama, trauma, and heartbreak and make a list. You know, ladies, the list. The list of all the attributes, traits, qualities, and deal-breakers we want in the man of our dreams. I feel prepared having this list. I feel excited having this list. I feel the Universe appreciates the practicality of me having the list and is creating the circumstances that will have me walk around the right corner at exactly the right moment to meet said lover, boyfriend, husband.

You want to see my list? Of course you do, and so does every man out there who could potentially have a crush on me. My list of what I desire, require, and am asking for in a partner is perfumed and soul-soaked with the energies of me and what is true for me. Giving you my list could possibly deprive you of the joy of what's true for you. I do think everyone should invest in the time to create their list. It provides clarity and intention to you and to the Universe. The small investment of time it takes pays off exponentially in your dating life. You always have choice, but it does make the yeses and nos so much easier. You can still take a detour if you're so inclined. You can swerve off the path of your dating purpose and have the fun of off-roading for a bit. But you will be aware of your choices and what they may create. You will have the personal leadership of your dating life from this moment forward.

I've had many dates since arriving in San Francisco. Some were appetizers: I tried them, and quickly and easily, decided a full plate was not for me. However, some were a main course, a recipe worthy of full consideration, worthy of eating with a dinner fork or maybe with no utensils at all. All in! As of today, there have been 18 first dates, only a couple of second dates, numerous conversations through email, phone, and text messaging, but only a few spectacular encounters. I have shared my soul (and, yes, my body) with only a few, very special, amazing men. And these amazing men, in all their manhood, have given me beautiful gifts. Gifts that have affirmed to me who I am, gifts that have validated my wants and needs, gifts that have moved me along my journey. Gifts that I hold very dear to my heart. It is with this intent of grace and gratitude that, one by one, I will share my stories of the selective few whom I have had the pleasure of unwrapping.

My Invitation to You

It's list time! It may be very tempting to do this with a group of friends, so let me hazard you with this question: will their thoughts and points of view affect or color yours? Will you have the space to be super vulnerable with yourself, allowing something that is uniquely true for you to come through? Clear, honest communication with yourself is the key here. Conversation, comparison, and collaboration with the ladies are not. Now is the time to get clear and state what YOU desire —whether it be a boyfriend, a spouse, a lover (or two) or a lifelong partner.

Your list can start with "I desire a life-long partner..."

And continue with "These are the things I require..."

"These are the things that are dealbreakers..."

And, "These are the things that I desire (the extra-juicy stuff beyond the requirements) to give, to receive..."

As for dealbreakers, whether it's no drugs, no small children, no crazy exes or something else, get real with what you're okay and not okay with. It's your life, and these things impact your daily experience. No one, really, truly, no one else is going to do this for you or be the guardian and advocate for this dream the way you can.

I admire, applaud, and appreciate your courage,
XO, Danna

---

* *Do you desire space to reflect and journal? Visit the "Invitation to Go Deeper" section at the end of the book.*

"Tis the most tender part of love, each other to forgive."
~John Sheffield

Chapter 6

Wrapped in Cargo Shorts and a Hawaiian Shirt: The Gift of Self, Freedom, and Forgiveness

*B*efore I can go forward, I must go backward. Back to a truly amazing man. Of course, he was amazing; he was married to me! Wink. Wink. He also witnessed my darkest hours, my deepest wounds, my nightmares that became my reality. And he walked with me through those places, over the uneven terrain, I believe, until I was safely on stable ground.

But that's not how it started. It started a very long time ago, almost two decades ago. I met Pat because one of my best friends was married to his first cousin. And we occasionally found ourselves thrust together in the same space, the same barbecue, the same pool party.

However, I was young (18) and so full of myself that there just wasn't any room for a "nice" guy. That was my "bad boy" phase. Let's just leave that for another time. And honestly, 18 was way too young, for me, to have any type of monogamous, serious relationship.

Starter Wife, Starter Life

Fast forward ten years, and you find me just having moved back to Tampa after three years in New York City. I was living in New York, climbing the corporate ladder, and feeding my unbridled need to live in a big city. But I did come back to Tampa. Back to family and dear friends. And back to learn one of the hardest lessons of my life. Pat had also just returned to Tampa after living in several other cities, and there we were, thrust into each other's lives once again.

Only this time, I had room in my heart and my newly purchased three-bedroom townhouse for a man. It was a long time ago and the details are fuzzy, but I'm pretty sure, and I think Pat would agree, that I came on to him. I was the flirty one. I was the aggressive one. I remember there was a big, tropical plant in my new backyard that I wanted moved. I mentioned this to him, and he offered to help me do the work. Okay, so yes, he did all the work. I probably made lemonade or something. And so the relationship commenced.

It moved quickly. We were living together within a month. We were engaged within six months. We were married the following year. It was a beautiful wedding of ivory and gold, in the evening, outdoors with lots of candles, with the reception at an old, southern house with a wraparound front porch lined with rocking chairs. We had our family, friends, great food, and the best wedding cake I have ever tasted in my life!

I jumped headfirst into this relationship, into this man. I followed my heart. Period. Not once did I stop to listen to my intuition. Not once did I stop to think about the traits and qualities that were Pat and if they were at all what I wanted or needed in my life.

How could I have known what I wanted or needed in my husband if I didn't know what qualities, traits, and attributes I wanted and needed in a partner? There was no list. Not then. Not even in my head. So, I followed my heart to a place of loving my husband deeply, passionately, and naively.

At 29 I thought surely I was mature and ready enough to be married. Today, at 39, I realize how ignorant I was of my own identity. I had never had a healthy relationship with myself, so it truly wasn't possible for me to have a healthy, romantic relationship with someone else.

Tender is the Heart

I look back on those ten years, and although I do see a lot of discord and a lot of difficulties, I also see a lot of compassion and a lot of tenderness. And a whole lot of stubborn loyalty and commitment. I see commitment to the sanctity of marriage. I see commitment to each other's needs. I see commitment to caring for and about one another. We truly did the best we could with who we were at the time. I think this is partly why we have come to call them "starter marriages," those first marriages for so many of us before we've come to know ourselves. Before we've asked the big, deep questions that move us dangerously close to the edge of clear and present self-love. Once we've walked that edge, the thrill of what's truly possible can, and often does, oust us from the safety zone of our commitment to a prior commitment.

I look back, and I remember my husband. Tall, rugged, handsome, a little shy, a little goofy at times, incredibly analytical, incredibly smart, incredibly in love with me. I see him waiting for me to go on one of our zillion errands (that I had created before I learned the value of simplicity), standing casually in his cargo shorts and Hawaiian shirt—the official uniform of Florida husbands.

I remember my husband summoning all his inner strength, strength I'm sure he didn't know he had, during those last difficult years when I was nothing but the empty box with barely the air of hope within me.

I look back, and I see my husband standing next to me at our dog's (Harley) bed in the ICU at the animal hospital, supporting me with a quiet strength that allowed me the courage to follow my knowing in deciding Harley's healthcare.

And I remember my husband taking the initiative to give Harley physical therapy by taking him swimming at his mother's house every day for weeks. This act of love, love for me, love for Harley, is what gave that dog the strength to walk again. Taking a step away from the whole starter marriage, clear and present self-love actualization; there is such beauty in a world where people can simply show up for one another, be present, engage and respond with...love. That never went unnoticed, unseen, unheard or, I hope, unacknowledged on my part.

Pat showed up in that act of love and a million other moments throughout our marriage, choosing over and over to show me love. Those million moments of choices that spanned the course of ten years together give rise to the auspicious power of love. A *Psychology Today* article said that love is as critical for your mind and body as oxygen. I agree that a gracious, kind love that connects you deeply to something bigger and greater than you is just that—as critical for your mind and body as oxygen. I would also say it nurtures your very being.

With that being said, it becomes almost nonnegotiable that when someone or something you love, that you are creating love with, is in need, is hurting so intensely, a power takes over to contribute to its wellbeing. Pat was that and more when our dog Harley was ill and we were desperate to ensure his best care and recovery.

After the death-defying illness, after not walking for three weeks from the loss of muscle and weakness, I will never forget the day I came home from work and Harley trotted down that long hallway and into my arms. My husband, my dear husband, is responsible for giving me one of the most loving memories of my existence. I will always be grateful to him for that.

I look back, and I see my husband sitting next to me on the ground, under the tree the day Harley died. He always said he had no idea how I had the strength to hold

Harley in my arms while the doctor silently ended his life. Oh, it's the same strength that he had to love me so much when I stopped loving him back the same way. It's the same strength that we both found within ourselves to learn and grow. The Universe was with us that day, and every day, holding our hands, having our backs, and silently walking us forward along that uneven terrain.

I remember the day, after being separated for six weeks, that Pat came home to find me there. Earlier that day, I was still at my friend Cindy's house, deciding if I should go back to my marriage, and Cindy's five-year-old daughter said to me, "Aunt Danna, do you miss Uncle Pat?" and I said, without hesitation, "Yes, I do." "Well then," she said, "go home." So I did. I went home to my husband to take the next step forward. Because at that time, I believed I could not walk forward without him.

And I remember walking together for the next year. Walking through grief, walking through fear, walking through humility, walking through pain, and walking through ignorance.

Side By Side

And we walked right into, and through, one of the most educational times of my life. We learned, together and separately, about ourselves, about relationships, about healthy behavior, about spirituality, about building a strong foundation. We went to individual therapy, marriage counseling, group therapy, and life coaching. We were both very committed to learning, and I was very determined to climb up from the bottom of the well, and so in true Danna intensity, I had placed self-help and spiritual books all over the house. They were in every room, on every surface, anywhere you looked, you could see one. My thought process was to surround myself with positivity and knowledge so I could pick up any one of these books, at any moment, and be able to take my mind to a brighter spot on the horizon.

During that year, we also traveled quite a bit. We spent two weeks exploring San Diego, San Francisco, and Denver. Then we spent another week exploring Portland. And another weekend in Denver. And a long weekend in Asheville. And in walking through each city, each step brought us closer to the truth. The truth that, at least for me, this man was not the right man for me. He was absolutely the right man for someone, just not for me.

And I remember the day my husband and I arrived on the other side of the street. He came downstairs and asked me (which I'm sure was extremely difficult for him to do) if I thought we could work this out, and with every ounce of strength in me, I said "No." And I remember that was the day my husband was no longer my husband. He walked out the front door and gave me back myself and my freedom.

The Single Lane

From that day forward, I was determined to do for myself, and if I didn't know, I was determined to figure it out. Some of it was pure obstinance. When Pat left, I realized that I had no idea when the garbage men came because he had been taking the trash out for ten years.

Well, I am stubborn and proud, and there was no way in hell I was going to call or text him to find out when the garbage men came. So I waited, and I watched. Finally, a few days later, they arrived, and I took the garbage out for the first time in ten years. I appreciate all the things Pat did to keep our household running, but it felt really good to be doing these things for myself, my way, for me.

This began the process of me living with more truth of me. Not a glamorous truth, but a truth where I took out the trash, learned how to clip the cat's nails, cooked dinner for myself, planned events with girlfriends, took care of myself when I was sick. Okay, there was this one time when I got really sick from eating bad food and called my friend Lynne to bring me ginger ale at seven in the morning. Thank you, Lynne. I love you!

My truth and freedom also included claiming Sunday as "Danna Day," later to become "Sacred Sunday." This was the day when I said no to everyone. Okay, no to everyone except Cindy and her family. I always loved them too much to ever say 'no' to family time with them. Other than that, it was no. So, what did I do on "Danna Day"? Anything I wanted. Sleeping in, wearing pajamas all day, grocery shopping, movie-watching, book-reading, attending church at First Unity in St. Petersburg, bike riding almost every Sunday evening along Bayshore Boulevard.

And when people ask me what I miss about Tampa, there really are only a few things. And you know what? They are all things I did on "Danna Day." And, I will add that I also miss all my other dear Tampa friends very much and am thankful for Facebook—to see snippets of their lives and families and children growing and creating.

The Power of the 'F' Word

Last weekend in my spiritual community here in San Francisco, Second Wind, we discussed the power of forgiveness. I joined this diverse group of men and women shortly after arriving in San Francisco. The group was chartered by a married couple, both former Seventh-day Adventist ministers. Our new center was a nondenominational spiritual community with some nods to their former ministry, meeting on and celebrating Sabbath, my favorite. We met weekly on Saturday mornings to gather as a community, eating, singing, laughing, and learning together. There was always time to connect and enjoy each other, along with a hearty convergence of sermon and conversation.

On this particular Saturday morning, we had watched segments from a documentary, *The Power of Forgiveness*. I had watched the documentary in its entirety previously with two of my new San Francisco girlfriends. It is a powerful documentary. Forgiveness is a powerful energy.

Then we were asked to pair up with someone and move through a forgiveness exercise. We were asked to look within for a situation that called for forgiveness. My immediate reaction was that I had no situations that needed forgiveness. My immediate reaction was arrogant. The arrogance, while staunch, gave way to the softness of my vulnerability. I was feeling the tug of inquiry, to go deeper. And that tug of inquiry required more vulnerability with myself. As the softness of vulnerability with myself took the place of arrogance, I looked again. I saw Pat. Funny, because we had each apologized to each other, each asked forgiveness and granted it to each other. But still, I saw Pat.

We began the forgiveness exercise. My partner went first, and we moved through her experience. What a vulnerable and enlightening thing to perform, in this case, with a practical stranger. Next was my turn. First, I had to describe the situation that called for forgiveness. What was showing up for me was that I needed to ask Pat for forgiveness for not acting on my decision and truth sooner, for wasting our time. Next, I had to pretend to be Pat and speak his thoughts. Hmmm, this is hard; if I could have known his thoughts when we were married, I'm quite sure our marriage would have been a lot easier.

Okay, so I took a minute, and in knowing this man for ten years, and in knowing our experience as "us" together, I knew the truth. That Pat understood this same thing, "us" together and our experience of learning and living and walking together to the other side of the street. That our lives were lived in the present of where we place our energy. Knowing where Pat is living in the present and where he is placing his energy, I know that Pat forgives me. And in the next step of acting as the relationship, I could see the beauty and grace that exists between us. I had just given myself permission to forgive … myself.

Pat and I have talked briefly since our divorce was finalized at the end of 2007. He now lives in Denver.

I am so happy for him. The first day we ever spent in Denver, I knew it was his city. I could picture him hiking, biking, and rafting. I could picture him building a life there in what felt like a smaller community with a more outdoorsy personality to it. More him. And, as much as San Francisco is my city, Denver is Pat's city, and I believe it will be the place where his spirit lives joyously. And that makes me happy—to simply know he chose a city that, from the moment we arrived, seemed to fit his tall, rugged body and laid-back love of life with its tall, rugged mountains and easeful living.

And in that spirit of living joyously, I remember my husband, Pat—an amazing man, tall, rugged, incredibly in love with me, wrapped in cargo shorts and a Hawaiian shirt, who left me with the gift of self, freedom, and forgiveness.

My Invitation to You

Getting jiggy with it! We (me, the mouse in my pocket, and any of you that are willing) are going to do a forgiveness and freedom exercise with all the men we've dated. Really. No, really. Jot them all down. If they pop into your head, write their name down!

Now, without having to walk down the minute and mind-numbing details of memory lane with each guy, ask yourself these questions for each name, and in asking the question, let's work on trusting our awareness, our gut, especially if you notice a pull, a tug, a hurt in your Universe.

- Truth, is there something here that I believe I need to forgive this man for?
  - No? Great, namaste, next question.
  - Yes? Then here are some more questions to play with to open the space: Is it still relevant? Can I acknowledge it's no longer relevant and let it go? (Big deep breath)

Was there an expectation that he act, behave, or respond the way you or a girlfriend would? (Men are men, not women, and we so often set ourselves up when we expect them to respond like women do.) Is it possible, he was doing the best he could, given the circumstances, his experiences, and the tools he had at the time? How has holding on to this affected my life? And, if I continue to hold on to it, will it decay or contribute to my life? Am I willing to let this go and allow the energies that have been locked up by this to loiter in my life and live in a sparkly, new way?

- Truth, is there something here that I believe I need to forgive myself for?

  - No? Great, namaste, next question.

  - Yes? Here are some more questions to play with to open the space: Is it still relevant? Can I acknowledge it's no longer relevant and let it go? (Big, deep breath.) Or was I possibly doing the best I could, given the circumstances, my experiences, and the tools I had at the time? How has holding on to this affected my life? And, if I continue to hold on to it, will it decay or contribute to my life? What would I tell my best friend if this was her and she was holding a grudge or grievance with herself? Am I willing to let this go and allow the energies that have been locked up by this to loiter in my life and live in a sparkly, new way?

I admire, applaud, and appreciate your courage,
XO, Danna

---

* *Do you desire space to reflect and journal? Visit the "Invitation to Go Deeper" section at the end of the book.*

" Encouragement: What the caterpillar calls the end of the world, the master calls a butterfly."
~Richard Bach

Chapter 7

Wrapped in a Black Cashmere Sports Coat and a Glass of Wine: The Gift of Excitement, Encouragement, and Harmony

I had been very impatiently waiting to start dating, but I had decided not to launch my Match.com profile until after arriving in San Francisco. I spent those first few weeks getting physically settled into my new home. My great, charming apartment above a boutique overlooking the hustle and bustle of 24th Street in Noe Valley. So, after facing hours of writer's block but refusing to get up from my chair until my profile was complete,

I was ready to turn on my profile. Okay, I wasn't "really" ready until I sent it to my closest girlfriends, and they put their stamp of approval on my profile as "genuine, authentic Danna." Then I was Ready.

Wow, it was like shoe shopping from the comfort of your couch. Oh, wait, that's Zappos.com, but you get the picture. Men of all ages, sizes, colors, and heights. Sporty, casual, dressy, functional, conservative, classy, funky. And like my favorite pair of Aerosoles shoes (bronze leather peekaboo toe with three-inch wood wedge heels), I wanted a combination of funky, sexy, functional, and comfortable. Yes, I am dreadfully sorry for comparing men to shoes, but girls "speak" shoes and what can I say, it's a clever analogy. You can turn this a million different ways, the fact is, tons of girls love shoes and spend a lot of time looking for and choosing that perfect pair. So guys, please be flattered that I am using this analogy. It's a twist on Cinderella— our "right" guy is that once-in-a-lifetime perfect (for us) pair of shoes that we will love, wear, and cherish forever.

Okay, enough about the shoes, I want to tell you about an amazing man. I received an email from my (yet to be known to me) amazing guy during my first week online. Something to the effect of, "I get down to the Bay Area about three or four times a year, would that work for you?" from a guy in Portland.

Portland. Portland, Oregon. I just moved to San Francisco. San Francisco, California. The city that *Forbes* magazine had just named as the best city for singles! And this guy from Portland was emailing me.

I laughed…out loud. Because of the distance, because of my strong, weird feelings about Portland, and because as soon as I saw his picture, I knew "something" was going to happen with me and this guy from Portland, Oregon. Did I mention my strong, weird intuitive nature?! It's a recurring theme. Here's the thing about my intuition: with many things, and with what seemed like every guy, I would have this knowing about him and the situation. It's like I would see images or a flash of information about him or us that, well, would energetically give me the whole story before it even began. And it was my choice to live the story and experience it's unfolding or just read the headlines in my mind's eye.

It's a 'Portland,' Folks

I'm going to digress and explain my strong, weird feelings about Portland. You need to know this! I have only been to Portland once. My ex-husband and I spent a week in Portland in February of 2007. I was still in the phase of trying to make things work, fit together, and so we went to Portland to check it out as a possible city to live. I chose February because I needed to be there during its most extreme month to see if I could handle it. Handle the weather that is. That was really my big issue with the city. And February is historically, scientifically, the coldest, wettest, grayest month. So, if I liked, or could handle, February, then maybe, just maybe, I could explore living in Portland. Ummm, let's just say that by the third day I wanted to kill myself.

The grayness, the wetness, the fact that I was there with my ex still trying to make things fit. And the thing is, I already knew, intuitively, that Portland was not my right city and that my ex was not my right person.

My friend Lynne recently came back from a trip to Portland (note: a summer trip) and said to me, "It's my city, I just feel it." I love Lynne, I know Lynne, and I believe that Portland could very much be her city, just like San Francisco is mine. It's the place where your spirit resonates and lives joyously. If Lynne moves to Portland, I have already solemnly promised her that I will visit…in the summer, of course!

For me, Portland represented (partly because of the season in which I was there) so much of what my home couldn't be: grayness, humidness, clouds that constricted my thinking and being, and a contrived sense of life (meaning I was trying to make it fit). I need mega amounts of clear blue sky; dry, crisp air; an environment that expanded my soul; and harmony with life and others. It became such a potent lesson for me and a repeated story with my friends that I coined the phrase, "It's a Portland" anytime I was referring to something that I wanted to work so badly but just couldn't fit together in my mind, my heart, my life.

On the flip side, I discovered some things in Portland that were so pleasantly surprising and touched me so deeply that I emailed a girlfriend halfway through my trip just to share them.

First, the people. The people of Portland are warm, easygoing, and incredibly friendly. These are people who not only say hello when you are walking down the street, but people who will, and want to, stop and have a chat. People who will not only give you directions but will walk with you a few blocks to get you to your destination.

Second, the food. The food in Portland is delicious, fresh, organic, and locally grown. When you eat in a restaurant in Portland, you can expect that the menu will not only offer yummy culinary treats but also provide descriptions of where the meat and produce were locally farmed. It was my first experience with eating at a restaurant and seeing on the menu where everything was sourced. "Sauvie Island Grower's Arugula & Radicchio Salad," "Stoneboat Farm's Fingerling Potatoes," "Reister Farm's Lamb Ragu," "Snake River Farm's Bavette." Do you see what I mean? You can probably taste what I mean! What a joy to see and experience.

Third, the very real sense of community. You can see it in the physical ban on big business and chain stores and restaurants. You can see and feel it in the mutual support residents provide to each other in raising their families and promoting each other's businesses. So my weirdness about Portland is also a strange affinity for the greenest, and grayest place I have ever seen.

Sure, a Guy 'Friend'

Okay, I think I've redeemed myself now with Portland, so back to my story of my amazing Portland man. After reading his short email and his short profile, I emailed him back, brazenly announcing my dislike of Portland. And so, the relationship commenced with emails, which very quickly turned into phone calls. He offered to cheer me up after my horribly bad first Match.com date with his own amusing bad date stories.

While I hesitate to share bad date stories, and I'm thrilled to say there have only been a few, this one is a mandatory share before I continue! So here I was, so excited to be in San Francisco and so excited to be dating, and the guy has me meet him 30 minutes across town, after knowing I was new to the area. I was a little disconcerted but embraced it as an opportunity to check out a new neighborhood. The "horrible" part was a conglomeration of the Mr. First Date Guy continuously attempting to hold my hand, a hand that did not want and was not ready to be held while also shuffling me to no less than three venues to, "see how I would react and respond to different environments." All sealed at the end of the evening with me doing the cheek turn when he attempted to kiss me. Ugh. And that's my bad first date in San Francisco. Now, let's continue.

All right, back to Portland and his offer to cheer me up after hearing about my bad date. Oh yeah, I took that hook, line, and sinker. Honestly, in the beginning I was thinking (at my friend Cindy's suggestion) that this guy could be a "guy friend"— someone to help me navigate through the beginning of my dating career. Ha. Within a few weeks, we had logged almost forty hours on the phone. And even though I had been on dates with other men, it was becoming very clear, very quickly, that I needed to meet this man in person.

Our phone conversations ranged from short and chatty—a quick hello, how's the weather, what are you doing—to long and engaging—when I was growing up this happened or what are your thoughts and feelings about xyz. We discussed every and all topics and began to create our famous "what if" scenario conversations. "What if I was really sick and I wanted soup from my favorite Chinese take-out, would you go get it for me?" That kind of thing. Fun. Imaginative. Connecting. I looked forward to each and every call. To hear his cheery, sunny voice. To hear that in "Shawn World" it was always 80 degrees and sunny, even though the Yahoo weather bulletin on my computer said that Portland was 40 degrees, rainy, and gray ... almost every day.

I was on a second date with a very nice guy, a handsome doctor who had a beautiful house literally a few blocks away from me in San Francisco, but my mind kept wandering north. North to a guy I had never met before except for hearing his voice 700 miles away in Portland, Oregon.

Shawn (often referred to as "Portland" because of the irony of the situation and because I have a brother with the same name) and I had already had a phone date. A few nights earlier, we ended up chatting on the phone for five hours. Finally, at about four a.m., we hung up. I remember thinking it was a great first date and that all that was missing was the first date kiss. It truly never occurred to me that we wouldn't be attracted to each other. It truly never occurred to me that we wouldn't get along. It truly never occurred to me that we couldn't spend hours together having fun.

And I would soon find out that I was right. I came home from that second date with the local guy and called Shawn to announce that it was time he got on a plane. Quickly. Like in a few days. He had already asked a few times if he could fly down so that we could meet in person, but I kept putting him off because of the distance thing. Although I had grilled him, asking him questions about his ties to Portland and very honestly and resolutely announced that if he didn't think he could ever move to San Francisco, then there was no reason for him to get on a plane and come visit.

The Plane has Landed

Five days later, on a Friday afternoon, he flew from Portland to San Francisco. Whew. Nervous. I was so nervous and excited and completely oblivious to the fact that anything could go wrong. At this point, with all the phone conversations, we were already calling each other "honey," and I already felt like I was in some sort of relationship ... yet to be defined.

It was like a scene from a romance movie. He was texting me with constant updates on his location. "At the airport." "On the plane." "Off the plane." "In a cab." "At hotel checking in." "On BART." (our mass transit system in San Francisco). "Off BART."

Oh My God! He was off BART! Which meant that he was walking up 24th Street toward my apartment. Holy Cow! I could feel myself standing side by side with The Universe watching its work unfold. Two people meant to meet and share their lives, for however long, for a purpose yet to be discovered. To say I was excited would be an understatement. I would love to say that I had little butterflies fluttering about in my stomach with sweet anticipation. Yeah, no, my adrenaline was pumping through my veins, I was sweating under my armpits, and I don't sweat, ever, and my mouth was as dry as the

Sahara. That's how excitement decided to show up in my body. Holy Cow! No, holy Sahara!

At this point, we were on the phone, and he was announcing the landmarks as he walked by them. "The gas station at the corner of Mission and Valencia," etc. Suddenly the lives of two people who lived 700 miles apart in two different cities in two different states who didn't know of each other's existence just three weeks earlier were about to collide. Then, he hung up. He said, "…works calling, gotta go." Huh?! What?! Seriously?! Right in the middle of this amazing love story scene you are hanging up for a work call?! See, this really isn't a fluffy romance novel; this is real life.

Then a few moments later, the phone rang again. Okay, a commercial break. Clearly not a big-screen romance, more like a made-for-TV movie. Nonetheless, it's my movie and still worth every calorie-laden, dripping-with-butter popcorn kernel. I walked downstairs and opened the door…and waited…for seconds that felt like hours.

New Beginnings

Then time disappeared, and Shawn appeared in my doorway…carrying red flowers, three red lilies. (That's what he was doing when he said work called, stopping to buy me flowers in my favorite color.) We smiled, we hugged, and we had our first kiss. One week after our first date, we had our first kiss. And it was a great first kiss. Totally in my first kiss hall of fame. Totally worthy of a big-screen movie star first kiss. It was that moment where the adrenaline pumping veins, sweating armpits, and dry mouth gave mercy to the delight of butterflies fluttering about in my stomach and the magic of desire being met on my lips.

We went upstairs to my apartment. I was so excited to show it to him after describing it to him on the phone. And he was excited to see it and to be there with me. We talked and kissed. We kissed standing up. We kissed with me sitting on the kitchen counter and him standing in front of me. We kissed sitting on the couch. A lot of kissing. I dare to say that kissing for me is possibly the most intimate of acts with a man. I get that the "other" things are very intimate, but technically you could do the "other" things without really being face to face, mouth to mouth, and kissing is about communicating the story of our energies for one another without ever saying a word. Who's with me on this? Ladies, you're either in the "kissing is the most intimate act" camp or well, you're not. I'll still be friends with you. 'Smiley face.' But I do love kissing my man, love it!

And phone calls. We each had to call our significant others (best friends, that is) to announce that, ummm, everything was okay and the person we met was actually a real live person that, yes, we liked and could spend the weekend with. For me, it was my friend Cindy. My voice of reason. The thinking head to my feeling heart. There would be so many more phone calls and emails with Cindy about Shawn and each of my amazing men.

Cindy is my very smart, practical, beautiful, full-out honest friend. We met the first week during our first "real career" jobs and have been friends ever since. We weathered the storm of pissy women making catty remarks to us, suggesting our looks got us our jobs rather than the same multi-day interview process we actually participated in, just like hundreds of other people. We shared countless guy stories and a neighborhood when we lived down the street from each other for eight years, each of us successfully purchasing our first homes as single women. I was one of the first people in the room when her first daughter was born, she was in my wedding and was my second home when I separated from my ex. We covered a lot of ground, a lot of laughs, and a lot of tears … and I couldn't imagine dating without her.

It seems weird now, looking back, after all my first dates. After so many "meet and greets" that lasted only an hour or so, that I was so sure and willing to spend the weekend with this guy.

We walked up the street to grab a bite to eat. We sat and lingered and enjoyed the space of lolling conversation and the novelty of being able to look at and touch each other. We strolled around my neighborhood. We came back to my apartment and strolled around each other.

When Shawn and I were discussing his trip, we agreed that he would make reservations at a hotel. However, we are all adults here, I very openly, maturely, and bluntly announced that if we got along in person as well as we did on the phone, then we both knew he wouldn't be staying in a hotel.

And so, that first Friday night, at around ten o'clock, we headed downtown to get some of his things from his hotel because he was clearly spending the night with me at my house. Most likely, like most of you, I was excited, curious, and a bit nervous. Although pretty confident it was going to be good, umm, great, there was still that little bit of unsureness until it actually occurred and was totally confirmed. Wink. Wink. So, all of that was stirring around along with dinner in my stomach. Not as light as butterflies fluttering, but certainly not anywhere near the day's earlier adrenalized response. What do we all feel when we know we're going to sleep with someone, and more explicitly, get naked and have sex with someone for the first time?!

We took BART, he grabbed a few things, we got my favorite coconut lemongrass chicken soup at my favorite noodle house near Union Square, and we headed back to my place. The next day, I took Shawn on a walking tour of San Francisco. Yup, I just did that, I fast forwarded you past the first-time sex with Shawn and transplanted you from the intimacy of my bedroom to the exposed public spaces of San Francisco! I'm leaving the details of first-time sex with Shawn with my memories—softly between the sheets.

Onward to the tour. It's a great tour because you get to spend the day walking through downtown, Union Square, Chinatown, North Beach, up to Coit Tower, down along the waterfront, perusing Fisherman's Wharf—all the great touristy San Francisco landmarks. We chatted along the way, stopped to snack, enjoyed the scenery, and really enjoyed each other's company. The tour came to a lingering close as we waited in line by Ghirardelli Square for the cable car to take us back to Union Square. We were tired from walking all day and not sleeping much the night before, and we stood together, me in front of him, leaning into him, leaning into whatever was to be, watching the sun set over the Golden Gate Bridge.

He retrieved the rest of his belongings from the hotel. We jokingly referred to it as "the condo" and went back to my home in Noe Valley. That night we had the first of our "date nights." We got dressed up and had a romantic dinner at a wonderful little Italian restaurant in my neighborhood. We talked. We talked. We talked. What did we talk about? Who knows! Everything. Anything that showed up. Life, love, everything in between, and all things weird and wonderful. It matters in the sense that we talked with so much ease and that we were covering all topics, light to serious. The actual content at this point? A blur of words and laughs. We drank a great bottle of organic wine that Shawn had chosen because he knew I preferred and appreciated organic food.

Sunday morning we got up…slowly. Come on ladies, if there's a hot man who looks like George Clooney (oh, yeah, I forgot to mention that part!) in your bed, are you jumping up for anything? No! You are not! You are going to savor it and snuggle into it. That's me, a Sunday morning snuggler. Refusing to acknowledge daylight, and in this case, refusing to acknowledge that our time together was almost over. Thus began the indulgence of my favorite spot.

My favorite spot was lying on top of Shawn. No, it's not what you're thinking…just wait a minute…wrapping myself around him, and hugging. God, he was the best hug. You know girls, the kind of hug where every cell of your body connects with every cell of his body and you just melt ... melt into each other ... melt into the moment. It takes your breath away by its sheer force, and then you breathe ... deeply ... and smile.

When we finally did get out of bed, Shawn went to get bagels, coffee, and the newspaper. We lingered over breakfast, and then we spent the rest of the day wandering around my neighborhood. We even checked out an open house. Oh, come on, ladies, who else knows this scenario to a 'T'? And who else knows the quiet wonder and hope of looking at an open house with a man you adore? Confession time—who's been there, done this, and throughout the tour was imagining you and said guy living together, picking out furniture, making dinner, making love, and making a life together? My hand is raised, how about yours? So fun. Thanks for playing.

It was the perfect Sunday.

Stops and Starts

Then I took BART with him to the airport. And this would become our ritual—me going to the airport to meet him and me going to the airport to see him off. I know I am an emotional person. But this, this is torturous, to be the only two people on earth melted into each other on a perfect Sunday morning, and then, hours later, to have to stand in an airport with thousands of people and kiss each other goodbye. Okay, I'm being a little dramatic. Just thinking about it boggles my mind, tugs my heart, and aches my body. I'm such a physical and affectionate person with my men. I mean the man that I'm with! If you're a Love Language person, my top by a longshot is "physical touch" followed by "quality time" and "words of affirmation." So, this situation really didn't align with that, but there I was. I never liked the idea of long-distance relationships and I was suddenly in one. Not liking the distance part and feeling like I had no control over any of it.

I remember the text message I got from Shawn as I left the airport in tears: it said, "I'm on the plane" and there was a frowny face emoji next to the words.

I called my friend Sandy crying. This was also part of the ritual, too: me calling Sandy from the airport when I was excitedly waiting for Shawn to arrive. And me calling Sandy in tears after I left him each time at the security gate. I could have called Cindy, but that would have required me to be honest with myself, and I wasn't willing to let go of my fairy tale yet.

This became the template for our relationship. The in-between time and the visits had a rhythm to them. A pattern.

We would talk on the phone pretty much every single day. I so looked forward to hearing that cheerful voice every morning. It's what got me going. It was my coffee. And it kept me moving forward in a time when I was drained from my recent journey into my new life. Every day was new. I had only been in San Francisco a month. I had no routine to my life, no structure, and only one local girlfriend. Thank goodness for that. And for my family here. But still, those phone calls and his voice and his words encouraged me each and every day to keep moving forward.

The visits always included me meeting him at the airport; taking BART together (he always got so excited about going on BART, it was very cute); exercise (walking together, Shawn going to the gym, me doing yoga); lots of talking; something touristy like taking the ferry to Sausalito or browsing The Ferry Building; date night (romantic, get dressed-up, walk to a charming, yummy restaurant on 24th Street, share a bottle of wine); enjoying breakfast together (Shawn getting bagels and making the coffee, me making bacon or Shawn's favorite apricot sausage, sitting and eating and reading the paper, some of it out loud to each other). We moved through the days so easily together. In all of these activities, we had a sweet, laid-back harmony in our time together. Until my experience with Shawn, harmony was an elusive thing. I always knew it existed and knew it was crucial in a successful romantic relationship, at least for me, but I had never experienced it until my time with him. For me, harmony is a consistency, cooperation, and amicability in being together in each encounter and across the dimension of the relationship. It creates a resonance, a fullness too that I love and appreciate beyond words. I feel like it sets you up to navigate the hiccups and storms with much greater peace. Having that harmony opened the space to focus and enjoy so many other things. Like the handsome man wearing the black cashmere sports coat.

It was during one of our date nights that Shawn wore the black cashmere sports coat. I remember when he bought it. He excitedly described it to me on the phone. I was jealous picturing him in Portland wearing it without me. Then a few weeks later, during one of his visits, he pulled it out of his suitcase. That date night he wore the black cashmere sports coat over a white button-down shirt worn casually outside of his designer jeans and black boots. Oh My! Handsome is an understatement. I already told you he resembled George Clooney, and now he was standing in front of me teasing me about how he heard the jealous tone in my voice when he told me about the sports coat, knowing the whole time he would bring it with him for date night. I can picture us together: him in that awesomely sexy, sophisticated outfit and me in a comparable sexy, sophisticated outfit—a black, low-cut wraparound shirt, a short denim skirt, black tights, and black boots with a black patent kitten heel. And I can picture us standing together at Bliss Bar on 24th Street enjoying the beginning of our date night at their monthly wine tasting. This month was all red zinfandel. My favorite. Juicy, strong, sexy.

One of my favorite days with Portland happens to have been one of our last days together. We woke up on a Saturday morning and headed out (and up the hill on 24th Street) on a four-mile walk along my street, down to the Mission, and back to my apartment. We stopped at Streetlight Records where Shawn bought a CD (we both had a thing for movie soundtracks—liked the variety of artists on them), then went up to my apartment and took an indulgent afternoon nap together. The new CD was playing in the background, the breeze was gently coming in the bedroom window, we slept lightly against each other. Looking back, symbolically not leaning too hard into each other or the future. We woke—me lazily, him energetically—but to our routine of great afternoon sex. There was a sweetness to this time that clearly stands out, that clearly was different. You know how I mentioned my weird intuitive nature? Well, I didn't mention this earlier, but there was a moment when we were in the living room talking about flights and visits, and it was the lightest, tiniest of feather whispers of awareness that this was the last visit. I blew it off, hard, in my mind and refused to hear it. I do wonder if my body heard it, perceived it, and was languishing in the time we had left. It wasn't the last time, but it still stands out in my mind. Feeling the coolness and crispness of the breeze across my body and the warmth and tenderness of Shawn's kisses across my face.

Late afternoon we picked up my Zipcar and headed north across the Golden Gate Bridge to my brother's house in San Rafael for dinner. We stopped at the grocery store, like I do each week, to pick up food for whatever my brother, his girlfriend, and I have collaborated on for dinner. Our family dinners are pretty much a weekly ritual for me, and I cherish them.

Shawn had never met my family. We had never been in a car together. We had never been grocery shopping together. We had never cooked dinner together. We had never spent time with kids together (let alone five-year-old triplets). We had never participated in an evening with other couples together as a couple. Every part of those five hours was completely new for us, and every part of those five hours was completely easy, fun, joyful … harmonious.

When we arrived home to my apartment, I headed straight for the tub and Shawn headed straight for the couch. I wanted to soak in a warm bath after a long day, and he wanted to relax in front of the TV for a bit. Typical, predictable, average couple on a Saturday night, you're thinking. Well, during each commercial break, Shawn would come into the bathroom, sit on the toilet while I lounged in the tub, and enthusiastically give me updates on the unfolding murder mystery being discussed on *60 Minutes*. Not typical, not predictable, not average—distinctive, surprising, endearing. A simple but extraordinary (for me) moment in time. Looking back across my life and across the malevolent memories, I always, always remember that I knew something different was possible. That there could be this loving, kind, and playful harmonious way of being and creating together. This day. This day showed me the actualization of that possibility as it played out across my life. I was grateful, astounded, and unassumingly arrogant in knowing it occurred.

The No-Return Flight

Shawn and I broke up a few weeks later. It was sudden. Or maybe it wasn't. Maybe I always knew, deep down, intuitively, that this man born and raised in Portland, Oregon had roots way too deep and wide to ever replant himself in a city that could not ever impart the nourishment that his city gave him to flourish and be "Portland."

Still, I was shocked. I think my friends were shocked. Maybe not. Maybe they were just shocked about how he all but disappeared from the Universe. At least my Universe. My body and heart were certainly in shock. I cried like a lovesick teenager. And yet I knew a long-distance relationship was a dealbreaker for me. But still, I had chosen it.

But after gallons of tears and gallons of chocolate ice cream, I found my heart. Sheltered but not closed. I found my spirit. Fractured but certainly not broken. And, I found my soul. Saddened but ever so grateful.

Yes, grateful. Grateful because this man wrapped in a black cashmere sports coat and a glass of wine left me with the gift of excitement, encouragement, and harmony.

My Invitation to You

From deal-breaking remorse to deal-breaking delight, let's shift some sh*t. Remember that list we worked on and created in Chapter 5? And, remember the forgiveness exercises we did in Chapter 6? Well, we are going to put them together like a celebrity couple mash-up. This is super simple: identify a time (in dating, in relationship) that you chose in opposition to a dealbreaker of yours. Now please let it go, forgive yourself, if needed, and move on if you haven't already.

If you're like me, you're an experiential learner with a zest for pleasure-seeking adventures. I certainly was during this time. So, what if you're not wrong for choosing a dealbreaker situation? What if you're never wrong for being you, living life and "learning" forward? This man, this chapter in my life, while clearly having one of my dealbreakers, also very clearly dealt me a winning hand in experiences that will continue to nurture my desires long into the future. Take those learning hands, hold them close to the chest, and let them nurture your desires long into your future love(s).

I admire, applaud, and appreciate your courage,
XO, Danna

★ *Do you desire space to reflect and journal? Visit the "Invitation to Go Deeper" section at the end of the book.*

"Passion kept one fully in the present, so that time became a series of mutually exclusive 'nows.'"
~Sue Halpern

Chapter 8

Wrapped in a Tie-Dyed T-Shirt and a Minivan: The Gift of Passion, Music, and Healing

A month after my relationship with Portland ended and four first dates later, I met Matt. Ummm, let me do the math: that makes him first date number seven. Whewww. I think I had looked at his profile, that maybe it came up in one of my searches, but I did not "wink" or email him first.

He emailed me. I was actually on first date number six when he emailed me. Hmmm, date number six, it might have been the local politician who during lunch sloshed down three martinis and continuously blurted out curse words. Umm, yes, that very well may have been it. I did retreat to the bathroom at some point and checked my texts in the hope of finding something to save me. Matt introduced himself and humbly said he didn't know if I'd be interested since he had three sons, but he hoped that I would be interested because he really enjoyed reading my profile. It reminded him of so many things he had taken for granted growing up in the Bay Area. It was a very sweet email. I found myself smiling while reading his email. That's a good sign. A very good sign. I also found myself smiling because as soon as I saw his picture, I knew "something" was going to happen with me and this guy with three kids who lived in the suburbs five minutes from my brother and the triplets.

So I emailed him back and, in my usual open and honest manner, stated that I had no problem with him having three kids, I was an aunt to five-year-old triplets who were guinea pigs to my parenting skills, it was just that I really wanted to have at least one child (with the right person). While I was married, we sort of tried to have kids by sort of not being careful, but my body sort of chose not to get pregnant. During that time, I contemplated babies. All my friends were piously popping them out, and it did tug at me from time to time. I thought my hesitation was with having them with my husband who became my ex-husband. Since I arrived in San Francisco to date, mate and marry, babies were in the equation.

The reason I brought this up was because his profile said that he wasn't sure if he wanted more kids and, well, I was definitely sure at that point I wanted at least one child. It's so weird to be talking about these topics before even going on a date, but that is the life of dating after a certain age I suppose, and it's certainly the life of dating when you know what you want.

He sent another email saying that he understood what I was saying and that with the right person, in the right situation, he could see himself having another child. Honestly, that lit me up. It sparked joy and excitement in me that opened the space of possibility. Then he sent another email that simply said something to the effect of, "...taking a chance here and giving you my phone number..."

I emailed him back and said something to the effect of, "...I'm a bit old-fashioned and think the guy should call the girl first" and gave him my phone number, but said this was easy because I was sure to answer or call him back. Thirty seconds later, my cell phone rang...and so the relationship commenced. Gotta love a guy who knows what he wants and takes action. We talked for a bit, then agreed to meet for lunch two days later in downtown San Rafael since I was heading over the bridge to have my weekly family dinner.

Bittersweet is My New Black

The Wednesday we met for lunch, the two days after our first phone call, was also Portland's birthday. It was also my brother's girlfriend's birthday, and my focus was on making her a birthday dinner along with being excited again about a first date. Honestly, the day was a little bittersweet. I did think about Portland that day. And I did miss him, still, just a bit. I missed our conversations, our daily connections, and the anticipation of our weekends together. But I was also excited about moving forward and excited about meeting Matt.

Being excited about meeting someone then actually meeting that person face-to-face and instantaneously realizing that there is a very strong, mutual attraction is, well, exhilarating. Okay, it's getting hot in here already and I haven't even begun to tell this story. Girls, this one might require a few cold showers in between paragraphs. Just letting you know!

So, we sat and enjoyed our lunch at a local Thai restaurant. And we chatted, and I listened eagerly to Matt talk about his three sons. This man was so in love with his kids; it was so apparent, so sweet, and so sexy. I remember he was talking about sports, coaching his son's baseball team, and I was thinking, "Okay, you don't know anything about baseball, not really, but pay attention, and learn, try to look like you know what he's talking about because you really like him and damn, he's hot…" After lunch, he offered to walk me back to my car, then asked if I would drive him the few blocks back to his office because he had walked downtown. We got into my car, and before I could even buckle my seatbelt, we were kissing. A kiss that had my heart racing so fast that I needed a seatbelt. The most amazingly passionate first kiss of my entire life so far.

Yes, my first kiss with Shawn was the perfect big movie screen first kiss, but this was the most amazing, dreamy, delicious, never-wanting-it-to-end first kiss! You know girls, your perfect kissing partner, the guy whose mouth, lips, tongue, style perfectly matches you in the most sensuous, tingle-down-to-your-toes way!

There was a second kiss. And a third. And then I drove him the few blocks back to his office. And a fourth kiss. Maybe a fifth. Finally, I left. I had errands to run—a birthday present to buy and groceries to pick up for dinner. My mind was numb, and I could barely remember how to drive the car. A few minutes later, I received a text from Matt, which totally confirmed my state of mind, "…totally incapable of rational thought…"

Double Dating

We agreed to have our second date that evening after my family dinner. This would be my first time having two dates in one day. There were about seven hours in between, so that makes it officially a second date, doesn't it? I was going to pick him up at his house, and we would go to downtown San Rafael to hang out. Yeah, sure, right, that's what I wanted to do. Hang out in some public place with this guy who when we stood near each other, you could almost see the sparks flying and could absolutely feel the current running between our bodies.

Not. Absolutely not what I wanted to do. I wanted to be alone with this man. I wanted to kiss him…just kiss him…for a very long time. So, seven hours later and many text messages about our mutual evenings, providing updates, we began our second date on the same day as our first.

Me: "at the grocery store," "preparing dinner," "eating dinner," "clearing the table," "leaving my brother's house."

Him: "at my meeting," "leaving my meeting,"
"what are you doing," "jumping in the shower," "here
whenever you are done." And so it went until I was
finally at his front door.

Yes, girls, I realize that I had just met this man, and
figuratively he was still very much a stranger. That's a
decision we've all been faced with. For women, simply by the sheer fact that men are (generally) bigger and
stronger, we actually do and must consider our safety.
And, quite frankly, I've rarely chosen what I chose with
Matt. But like Portland, I knew intuitively that I was
meant to be in this place with this man.

Have you ever just known something to be true?
Maybe it came with a lightness in your body, in your
world, versus the heaviness and contraction that comes
with something being a lie for you, but you knew and
chose from that knowing. Oh my God, sidebar: keep
doing that! Keep checking in with your awareness and
knowing, keep choosing from and for what is true for
you. No one else can do it for you, so please, please keep
doing it! I knew intuitively that I could trust this man,
just like I trusted Portland, with my heart, my body,
my soul.

And our second date was exactly what I wanted our
second date to be: hours of kissing. Hours of the most
amazingly sensual, arousing, passionate, sexy kissing.
I had changed the reservations on my Zipcar before I
left my brother's house, knowing my intentions for the
evening. Okay, so there was more than kissing. At some
point, shirts came off, and I remember some deep, sexy
sighs coming from Matt at the sight of my navel ring and

my tattoo (the former of which I no longer have, because at some point, my body was done with that fad).

What was so sexy about Matt's body? What's so sexy about any man's body that we adore and desire? His physique. His demeanor. His interaction with the world and me. His biceps, his body in those jeans. His smile and eyes delighting in me. That. And a million other things that made it so. I also remember there was a movie playing in the background, which at some point got turned off and music turned on. From that moment forward, there would always be music playing whenever Matt and I were together. Literally, not some figuratively mushy reference here.

Irrational Choices

About an hour before I needed to have the Zipcar back, I looked at Matt and said, "If you didn't have to work tomorrow, I would so take you home with me…" He said, "Let's go." And so he followed me back over the bridge to San Francisco. It was around one a.m. The night was cool, crisp, and clear, and we were delirious with arousal and dehydration. Seriously, we had been making out for like five hours. Gatorade had officially become a staple in my house when I met Matt. This was before coconut water became a thing. Today it would be coconut water or watermelon juice. I'm a bit more health conscious and selective with my beverages these days. I was nervous but very comfortable with what I was doing. I had come to the decision that if the Universe was bringing us together for amazing sex, then so be it. I truly had no idea it would be so much more and was truly okay with whatever the outcome. The Universe was standing there with passion as thick and blinding as the San Francisco fog, and I walked into it, disappeared into it, breathed it into every pore in my skin.

By the time we got to my apartment, it was about two a.m. Considering he had to leave at six a.m. to head back across the bridge, and the activities of the night, I think we got about two hours of sleep. I remember asking him the next day if it was beautiful driving over the bridge so early in the morning, and he responded with a full description. And so began many exchanges of questions, deep thoughts, philosophic, poetic descriptions (of nature, sex, life), our daily life, discussion of problems we were each facing, sharing of successes and special moments we each experienced. Those conversations became a ribbon that intricately wove its way through my days and through our time together.

Our third date was planned for two days later. The thing about our dates is that there was usually one or two a week. Matt had a very full schedule with work, having his kids, coaching their little league team, etc. But I compromised and embraced the time we did have together. And when we were together, Matt was completely with me. Our dates were precious, appreciated, and timeless—meaning I never looked at the clock. I was so in the moment, so totally consumed by our togetherness and our nakedness.

We went out to dinner on our third date. Actually, a few minutes after he walked in the door to pick me up for our third date, we were ripping each other's clothes off…then we went out to dinner. After dinner, the clothes were ripped off again. Oh, and one more time for good luck!!! Matt left that night around midnight. We were both just glowing and giddy and so content.

I remember, ummm, during the moment of, ummm, "consummation" Matt looked down at me and asked if I was okay because I had a look on my face. I'm smiling now thinking about it. I explained that look to him the next day in an email. "... you know when you are about to eat a yummy hot fudge sundae and you know it's going to be so ridiculously good and you take that first bite and you have total confirmation that it's so ridiculously good? Well, that's what that look is, the moment of total confirmation that it's (the sex) is so ridiculously good..." He laughed and said he looked forward to seeing that look many more times, and I was so ready for him to see it again. The first week we actually got together three or four times because he was about to go out of town on vacation with his kids for 11 days. And because we just couldn't get enough of each other.

There was a lunch, which by the time the hour arrived we had already decided to eat in. Our emails were steamy and suggestive and, honestly, why waste time in a restaurant when we could eat in my apartment and spend the rest of the time naked?! Cindy had already told me that she thought he was a time-waster. Cindy, my voice of reason. There is no reasoning to be had when you are in the midst of the most amazing, passionate sex of your life (so far). And so, I told Cindy, "If this guy wants to adore every square inch of my body, why, why would I not want that?!" Seemed like a great way to "waste" time. I had no idea what this relationship would be for me, but I was willing to leap off the cliff of "no idea" and find out.

Let's see, the day we had lunch, we also had a late afternoon snack. Seriously girls, the most amazing sex! It was like our bodies knew each other in some other space and time and had found each other again after being separated. It was truly a force of nature. I could not be in his presence without radiating sexual energy, without touching him, without kissing him, without wanting him in the most biblical sense, and being naked within minutes. This was inevitable and consistent every single time we saw each other. Okay, except for the time he hurt his back and could not physically move.

Taking a cold shower break. Be right back.

Irrational Desire

Okay, I'm back. But Matt, he's in Palm Springs on vacation with his kids. I was happy for him. He worked hard and was so active in his boys' lives, he really deserved some rest and relaxation. However, my body craved him so intensely while he was gone. I counted the days until he came home. We talked every day. Either on the phone, or by email, or text messaging. Our conversations and us together in whatever forum were always so open, so honest, so vulnerable, so free, so intense, so sensual, so sexy, so flirty, so engaging, so supportive.

One night while Matt was on vacation, I watched a movie. No big deal, it was *You've Got Mail*. I've seen this movie a dozen times. I love romantic comedies. However, this time I noticed something in the movie I had never noticed before. Music. There was a beautiful soundtrack to this movie, and I had never really heard it before. Before Matt came into my life with his love of music, his talent for playing the guitar, his joy in singing. He had already played for me (over the phone) a few times. How sweet it is to be serenaded by a hot, sexy guy before going to bed. What sweet dreams. So as I watched this movie, I texted Matt and told him about this new revelation, and I thanked him for bringing music back into my life.

By the time Matt was on his way back home, we had exchanged some very intimate discussions, thoughts, feelings, and pictures. Oh yes, I created a very special game for his car ride home. "Name The Body Part And What You Are Going To Do To It." The way the game was played was that I sent pictures I had taken of myself (snippets really of various body parts) and then he would text me back the name of the body part and what he was going to do it. Oh, Good God, I need another cold shower.

Because it was so much more than sex, it was this unspoken erotic, deep, warm connection. I could feel the distance, and the closeness, whether it be physical or emotional. I was connected to it like the invisible communication line that connects two cell phones. I remember the day his vacation ended, and he was on his way back home. I emailed him that morning (before our infamous car game) and told him that I was sorry that his vacation was ending but so glad he was coming home because I needed him ... needed him next to me, on top of me, in me. Wow, this is hard to share. And he emailed me back and said, "I feel exactly the same way." Deep breath. One more. Okay. I can continue now.

Fuchsia Flags

This man had some fuchsia (Cindy and I agreed on
fuchsia instead of red) flags for me in what I wanted for
myself. For what was on my "list." But yet I was willing to take the detour. I was willing to travel down this
road, totally unaware of the destination, because I felt its
overwhelming healing powers. I'm not sure what part
of me it was healing. My heart, my soul, my spirit, my
body. And it wasn't necessarily the sex that was healing;
it was the in-between time. The laughing and talking
and sharing and touching in between the sex. It was in
between that we nurtured something very deep within;
it was in this place that there was healing.

We were lying in my bed one night, "in-between,"
and Matt told me his story about God and the butterflies. In previous years, difficult years for Matt when he
questioned God's existence in his life, his existence at
all, he told me that in those darkest moments, something began to appear. It was butterflies. Butterflies that
weren't native to the area. Butterflies that shouldn't have
been there but were, fluttering around him, announcing the presence of God's love. In these moments over
the years when Matt questioned God, his butterflies
would appear. He cried as he told me this story. This
strong, sexy, rugged man. And as I sat there naked in
my bed with him, I looked around my room and saw all
the butterflies. No, I wasn't hallucinating. You see, my
pillow shams have butterflies fluttering about. My window has a string of butterflies hanging from the curtain
rod... fluttering about. My shower curtain in the bathroom has butterflies fluttering about. My little table in

my foyer has appliqued butterflies fluttering about. Even my mouse pad is a butterfly. Enough said. In that sweet, deeply emotional, vulnerable moment, I was in absolute peace in knowing that this man and I were supposed to be exactly where we were at that moment in time.

I never turned my Match.com profile off while we were together. I knew that Matt was still dating, and although I really had no desire to date, I did push myself on a few. But I realized I was so not into it and truly it was not fair to anyone I was going on a date with. I later learned that Matt experienced the same thing. One Sunday night, after a particularly bad date that I thought was going to be a really good date, I emailed Matt. I very cryptically said something about having a disappointing evening. Matt instinctively knew me so well that he offered up the platform to speak about 'it." I figured it was time to open *the* can of worms. I talked about the bad date and the fact that I had gone on a few dates but was not really opening myself up to meeting anyone.

Matt emailed me back the next morning to tell me that he was also having integrity issues with the situation. And that he was experiencing the same thing when going on dates with other women, and had cancelled dates because of our situation. He also said that he didn't want to be the obstacle that kept me from connecting with someone else. Okay, you are confused, yes, I can see that. Let me explain further. You're thinking, why would you want to date other people, and why would Matt want to remove himself as an obstacle from you connecting with other men? Well, because Matt had been very seriously and intently looking within himself to navigate through his feelings about having another child. He had spent weeks struggling with this, discussing this with his closest friends, and now was sharing with me that, no, he just couldn't see himself having another child.

Ouch. This was painful. This was crushing. This was the moment I realized my true feelings for this man. By the time he called, I was crying and I was angry. Angry because I asked this question before we ever went on our first date. Just like I asked Portland if he could relocate to San Francisco before we ever had our first date. So, yes, I was asking the questions and being very intentional about my choices. But I have to look inward here. Intuitively I knew the answers to both of these questions without ever having to ask them aloud. So really, who was I angry with? This is another situation of choosing the experience over avoiding the ending. Think of some wonderfully heart-torn romantic drama where you know the ending— there is death and despair and gut-wrenching heartache, but you watch it anyway because the journey, the story, is so beautiful you cannot bear to not have it in your life. That's what I'm talking about here. My crazy intuition and knowing, if I had been willing to ask more questions and have the awareness, would have instructed me to skip the story and the dreadful ending. But the story, I had to have that beautiful story. Without it, there would have been an empty space where there is now music.

Slow Burn

It took Matt and me a week to break up. Because we really didn't want to. Because we liked each other so much.

Because we cared about each other so much. Because we were so undeniably attracted to each other and enjoyed all of each other so much. I just couldn't fathom this man not being in my life, and yet, I didn't know how to move into friendship with him. I didn't know how to turn off the passionate chemistry. How to not want to kiss him or touch him. I just didn't. And so I prayed and I cried. I cried for this great loss. For experiencing, in an instant, the complete, overwhelming potential of what could be mixed with the complete, overwhelming loss of what would never be. It was painful.

Yes, part of me was in pain just thinking about being physically separated from Matt. I mentioned earlier that I am a huge physical touch person with my partners, and my body connects so deeply with them that there really is a physical reaction to that withdrawal. To that forever separation. Part of me was freaking out about losing the best sex I have ever had so far. And part of me was in so much pain because I had come to know a man who had values as deep as mine. Integrity, compassion, and kindness so strong that he was willing to walk away from this amazing union because he cared about me. Because he wanted me to know motherhood. Because he could not take that dream away from me. Whewww.

Our last time together was symbolically and ironically on Mother's Day. I spent the morning at Glide Church with a girlfriend. Glide has amazing music. Strong, powerful, soulful music. And that was what I needed. In the afternoon, Matt picked me up from my girlfriend's house, and we went back to my apartment. He was wearing jeans and a tie-dyed T-shirt that day.

He looked so...so Matt. Sexy, unpretentious, cute, relaxed, present. We talked. I can't even remember the words. I just remember being so close to him and, unlike every other time, we weren't naked within minutes. We weren't consumed with each other for hours. We were trying to talk, to make sense of things.

Did we end up having sex? Yes. God, yes! Matt looked at me and said, "I want to kiss you so badly." And I said something about wanting to have sex with him because, well, it was us, and I didn't know how to not instinctively want and need to be with him, be naked. We had sex. It was different this time. Still amazing. But different. Maybe our bodies, maybe our souls, knew it was the last time. As Matt lay on top of me, he looked into my eyes, and with tears in his, he said, "You cannot fall in love with me."

The next morning, I woke up knowing what I had to do. I prayed, and this is what I found. That I had to let Matt go. He had shown me integrity, compassion, and kindness with his vulnerability, honest conversation, and caring for my wellbeing. He knew (at the time) I wanted kids and wasn't willing to string me along for his own desires to keep me from mine. Now I had to do the same. I had to relieve him of his angst. We cared enough, so much, about each other that it was the right and only thing to do.

But when I prayed, I also found this...that this man who drove a minivan with three kids and lived in the suburbs, who was wrapped in jeans and a tie-dyed T-shirt, left me with the gift of passion, music, and healing.

My Invitation to You

$\mathcal{J}$t's a beautiful thing to acknowledge the serendipity of the Universe bringing people into our lives to expand it, heal it, and ignite it. It's a very beautifully empowering thing to ignite our own flames. This exercise helps us fan our own flames, feed our own joy and desires. And we can utilize our men, what we've received from them, as the kindling.

In the center of a piece of paper, write down one of your guy's names. Now, form spokes out from there with gifts you received from him (music, excitement, freedom). Then create arrows (sparks) from each gift, and identify at least one activity or thing you can do or add to your life that creates that same thing/feeling for you. You'll end up with a bonfire of possibilities for fueling your life.

> *I admire, applaud, and appreciate your courage,*
> *XO, Danna*

---

* *Do you desire space to reflect and journal? Visit the "Invitation to Go Deeper" section at the end of the book.*

"It is only in adventure that some people succeed in knowing themselves – in finding themselves."
~Andre Gide

Chapter 9

Wrapped in Sneakers and a Cup of Tea: The Gift of Clarity, Adventure, and Friendship

*J*think it was just a week or so after my relationship with Matt ended that I pushed myself off the
couch, out the door, and on a few more first dates. Okay,
it was more than a few dates. It was five first dates in one
week. It was me trying to show the Universe that I was,
and wanted, to move forward, and it was me just trying to
refocus. I briefly ignored my lessons and my intuition. If
I had been paying attention to any of what I had learned,
I would have known it was not in my best interest, or the
best interest of the guys I met, to actually meet them. All

except one. And that would be Brian. Brian was first date number eleven.

I came across his profile in one of my searches, found it interesting and intriguing, and emailed him. His profile was smart, witty, and long-winded. I enjoyed reading it. I enjoyed how his writing engaged me. He emailed back pretty quickly. Something about describing my Pisces characteristics: if he was right, we should meet for tea, and if he was wrong, we should meet for whiskey. Or maybe it was the other way around. Regardless, his wit and wisdom made me smile.

And, yes, I was smiling because I knew "something" was going to happen with me and this mysterious, quirky guy.

We agreed to meet for tea at Martha Brothers Café near my house on 24th Street in the middle of a Tuesday afternoon. And so, the relationship commenced. I remember when I met Brian—he talked fast, was a bit wired, was juggling lots of activities in his life, but incredibly focused and genuine during our time together. I think I will always have that vision of Brian—hyper, multi-tasking, driven, kind, caring, attentive, and always willing to keep on talking. He just has this very open and obvious affinity for great, challenging, intensely engaging, philosophical, spiritual conversation. Brian always leaned left with his conversations. Well, actually way beyond left, more like off the grid to Buddhism and Sufism and astrology and the big philosophical question of "why are we here?" It's awesome to be a part of this kind of conversation.

And so, as we sat outside of Martha's on a bench in the well-above-average weather for May in San Francisco, we talked. Brilliant blue skies, quiet air, temperatures in the low 80s and no sight of Karl, our famously known resident fog, laid out the perfect afternoon for tea. We talked and got to know each other, but it wasn't the shallow basics. It was put your scuba gear on and dive right in talking. The big catch of the day was one simple question that propelled my mind 20,000 leagues under the sea. (That's my Pisces analogy, my "fish in water swimming two directions" analogy. I am allowed one Pisces analogy, aren't I? I'm done now. Let's continue with the actual story.) The question was, "What are your top five priorities in life?"

Ummmmm. Uhhhhhhh. Wait a minute. I know the answer to this. I swear I do. I am a very introspective, intentional, spiritual person; I absolutely know the answer to this. Or do I?! Hmmmm, I could not articulate them. Me. Miss Articulate more often than not. Maybe it was the extraordinary May heat. Yes, I know I'm from Florida, but in Florida if it's above 75, you are either in your air-conditioned car, your air-conditioned office, or your air-conditioned home. You are always climate-controlled. My life in San Francisco was solely controlled by Mother Nature—whatever she brought that day is what I experienced. No recycled, stifled air. No constant 78 degrees. The only thing constant about the weather in San Francisco is you know that it is constantly changing, possibly by 20 degrees in 20 minutes.

Left Turn

See, it's not that I couldn't answer the question, it's that my mind decided to take a left turn on one of the many

San Francisco streets that specifically says, "No Left Turn." Brian and I enjoyed our tea and our conversation. But I was left still traveling west after taking that left turn, and I was trying to find a road that would bring me back to that place in me where I absolutely knew the answer to the question, "What are your top five priorities in life?"

Later the same day, I read the weekly e-newsletter from my church and there it was again, this time in print: "What are your top five priorities in life?" And then, "Are you focused on them?"

Oh Boy! Now I had been tasked to not only identify them but be focused on them. Let's just say I started freaking out. Like I didn't get enough air when I dove the 20,000 leagues under the sea to search my soul for the answer. Too many air bubbles and I was having a little freak-out moment. So, what do I do at ten o'clock at night when I'm having a little meltdown? Well, I send frenzied emails to my incredibly supportive and caring life coach whom I had found in San Francisco just a month earlier. And since I had an appointment with her the next day, I thought I would just inform her that my life was in shambles and I had no idea what my priorities were, let alone if I was "working" on them.

I told you I could be dramatic. However, by the next day I regained my composure and my articulate voice. My coach and I had worked through the challenge to a place where I not only identified my priorities, but fully acknowledged and praised myself for very actively working on all of them in a balanced and intentional manner. Of course I'll share them with you. After all that, you think I wouldn't? My top five (actually seven) priorities in life are: to find a great partner and build a relationship; to continue my career in an environment that provides challenges, respect, balance with the rest of my life; to continue to find creative outlets for my artistic side; to spend time with my family; to continue to build and deepen new friendships while also maintaining existing ones across the country; to focus on a healthy, active, outdoors lifestyle; to participate in, and have an intentional experience, in a spiritual community.

Rules of the Road

The importance of knowing this is not so that I could hold up my end of the conversation when someone asked me the question or to have the right or correct response to a survey; knowing the answer is knowing myself. Knowing and actively participating in my priorities is the Universe knowing that I am authentically me. This clarity helps define me every single day in every single situation that comes to me. And it simplifies my life immeasurably because if something comes to me or is asked of me that is not in alignment with my priorities, well, it's easy to identify and easy to say no to if I so choose.

A few days later, I had my second date with Brian. It was a progressive occasion of conversation, eating, and drinking wine. It started with him picking me up at my brother's house in San Rafael and continued west along the winding country mountain road through West Marin to Pt. Reyes with a continuous stretch of conversation, food, and wine. This has always been, and will probably be, one of my favorite excursions. Talk about driving through one of those exquisitely filmed romantic movies. This parcel of land is truly one of the most magnificent in the world. Winding roads meet gold straw hills speckled with black and white cows, bright, shiny manes of horses with land opened only by swathes of blue inlets until the ocean explodes into your vision! The food brings the same intensity of awe and yum. Most of it coming right from the land beneath it: cheese creameries, oysters harvested ten feet away, wine from grapes you can eat off the vines in front of you, and the smell of freshly baked bread wafting through the air. Whenever someone asks me why I moved here, this is why. This land and abundance of life is why. It is religion for me. The conversation continued in unity with the road we traveled through the mountains—organic, spiritual, and winding.

After our second date, I asked Brian if we could be friends. At the time, because I just couldn't picture "it," a romantic relationship with Brian, that is. Funny, because I am such a visionary in so many ways, realizing that you have to allow yourself to know that things don't always become what we imagined, but they still become what we need or want. But still, because I couldn't wrap my mind around this vision, I dismissed it quickly. Too quickly. Now, looking back, I realize my quick dismissal was caused by pain and fear. The pain my heart was feeling in breaking up with Matt and my fear of losing another amazing friendship.

And so we continued our relationship in friendship. A friendship that was caring and kind and sweet. A friendship that gave us space to go off and live our lives and come back together to explore. After not seeing my friend for about six weeks, we got together on a Friday night to catch up. Only for Brian and me, catching up is not a sprint to the finish line; it is a marathon of cross-country stature. When Brian picked me up, our Friday night conversation started at my apartment at six p.m., across the Golden Gate Bridge to Marin, at a barbecue with Brian's good friend in San Anselmo, back into the city, over tea in my apartment, finally ending when we fell asleep...talking...at about four a.m. We woke a few hours later, talking like there had never even been an interruption in the conversation. It finally did end, a few hours later, after breakfast. Cindy and I discuss everything—life, her kids, my dating, etc.—and in partially explaining my relationship with Brian to Cindy, a mother of three, I simply said, "Brian and I together are like two kids on a playdate—we don't stop until we are physically removed from each other's presence."

Drinking and Driving

Two weeks later, after Brian had returned from a long trip and I had returned from a morning of volunteer work at the food bank, we began our next adventure, an amazing adventure for me. It started with an invitation from Brian to get together for margaritas. After accepting this invitation, I looked at my friends I had just finished eating lunch with and said, "Brian and margaritas are a dangerous combination." A dangerously fun combination that I knew would bring much joy and little sleep. So, we talked and giggled over one margarita that became three along with oysters and paella at Fresca right down the street from my apartment. There was some talk about driving to Marin to meet Brian's friend for a concert, but seriously, after three margaritas, driving is just not an option. So, we continued our conversation and giggles late into the evening.

The next afternoon after church, I walked up the hill to Brian's apartment where our time together reconvened, we ate lunch, and derailed my anxiety attack over breaking my phone. A very possible result of the three margaritas from the night before when I dropped it. I generally don't talk on the phone when I'm visiting with friends and love the opportunity to check into the timelessness of a journey with Brian, but I was also in the middle of managing a house repair project for a friend and was still trying to form a cohesive plan of action. After a quick trip to the Verizon store, I had full connection to my world again, if needed. Luckily, my world that Saturday afternoon only needed to consist of Brian and me, driving back along our winding country road to West Marin. Past horses, cows, sheep, deer, and turkeys, and surrounded by pale straw-colored rolling hills, towering dark green sequoias, the brightest clear blue sky, and meandering creeks that opened themselves into pools of glass that reflected nothing less than a miracle. The sheer miracle of awe-inspiring beauty. This is so why I love it here—because I can be driving down a winding country road in a pickup truck listening to music and experience God or spirit just as surely as when I sit in church and pray or when I'm walking along a city street and am struck by the charm of my life. And the charm of my friendship with Brian because he so gets this and because, in our adventures, we get to experience it together.

Our trip out to West Marin was with intention. The intention and goal of purchasing fresh oysters for a barbecue at a friend's house in San Anselmo that evening. Along with our freshly picked oysters, we dined on salmon caught by Brian's friend's daughter during a recent trip to Alaska. Pair that with fresh vegetables, a crisp sauvignon blanc, and wonderful company, and you have a delightfully chic and spiritual barbecue that is very California. And very much me getting to live out the discussion from church that very morning about spirituality and food. About acknowledging every action, and person, it took to bring our food into being and onto our plates.

The adventure picked up again, after a brief Sunday intermission, on the morning of Labor Day. During our three-margarita dinner on Friday, I had discussed with Brian my thoughts about the house repair project I was hired to manage. The person who hired me is not only a friend of mine in Florida, but also one half of the team that stayed with me during my first week in San Francisco to help me clean, paint, and physically move into my new home. And here was this person, hiring me to manage a house repair project for her sister's house about ninety minutes north of San Francisco in Santa Rosa. This person wanted to pay me, and because I was unemployed at the time, I accepted this job. Additionally, we had the opportunity to hire a contractor to complete the work with his work crew requiring very little involvement from me. My dilemma with this situation is that I didn't feel right about accepting money to help a friend who was trying to help her sister (begin to dig herself out of a dire situation) or about hiring a contractor that, although very competent and fair, would still cost my friend way more than she had anticipated spending. In friendship, Brian challenged me to think of another solution. And in friendship, Brian offered to give his time, his skills, and his amazing spirit to spend the entire Labor Day working on this house project. And so I spent Labor Day with the homeowner, another friend of mine who volunteered his time and skills, four paid day-laborers, and Brian, living out the meaning of the day, the spirit of community, and experiencing God/spirit once again in kindness and love.

In kindness and love, this memory will live within me. Of course, I thanked Brian, and my other friend, for helping me and a complete stranger that day. But what I really thanked Brian for was just being his amazing self. And in spending time with Brian being his amazing self, I am more me, a better me. I was always comfortable with myself around Brian and felt that warm, welcome space of no judgment which simply allowed me to be my vulnerable, fun, quirky self and that always perpetuated itself into sharing and baring more. Those choices, easy choices, allowed me to be a better me. What kind of friend helps you be a better person yourself? One that you just can't imagine not having in your life.

Four days later, I found myself sitting cross-legged across from Brian on the floor of his living room, drinking a decadent pinot noir at 11:30 at night, and listening to some very soulful music. In kindness and love, I floated into the possibility of being and knowing I was exactly where I was supposed to be at that moment. All my experiences with Brian were fun, easy, and enlightening in some way. I think our relationship is very Buddhist; we just are. In the moment, in the conversation, in the realm of possibility that anything is game and anything can be challenged. Okay, not sure if that last part is very Buddhist-like, but you get the idea. It just was.

And in "being," I found that Brian, this mysterious, quirky guy wrapped in sneakers and a cup of tea, gave me the gift of clarity, adventure, and friendship.

My Invitation to You

In your adventure of living, what are your top five priorities? Come on, you knew that was coming! And, truly, what I know for sure is that by knowing these and reconfirming them every so often, everything in my life has become easier. Why? Because I can easily say yes to things that nurture my priorities and no to things that don't or at least be very aware of my choices. Get ready for more ease in your life. You're welcome.

I admire, applaud, and appreciate your courage,
XO, Danna

★ *Do you desire space to reflect and journal? Visit the "Invitation to Go Deeper" section at the end of the book.*

"The elegance of honesty needs no adornment."
~Mary Browne

Chapter 10

Wrapped in a Flannel Shirt and a Guitar: The Gift of Romance, Honesty, and Inspiration

It had been a while since I had been on a great first date. You know the kind that you get really excited about—butterflies in the stomach, annoying your girlfriends with constant chatter about the big event, the must-have new article of clothing to make the perfect outfit. So here I was, ready to have that great date, but it took me a little while to get to it. Actually, my last great first date was Matt, and that was three months earlier. You know, Mr. "'Wrapped in a Tie-Dyed T-Shirt and Minivan." I had emailed Tom weeks earlier, yes, another Match.com guy. And he emailed me back pretty quickly. Gotta love a guy who sees what he likes and takes action.

Unfortunately, I was feeling a little disheartened by recent dating, and I just wasn't prepared to go on a date until I could feel excited—it just wouldn't be fair to me or the person I would be going on a date with. So I took a little downtime for myself, and then emailed him back with my phone number. Okay, Cindy also prodded me to go out with him. She read his profile and thought he was a great fit for me because of his corporate job, his intelligence, looks that she knew I liked, and musical tendencies, which she knew I loved. Basically, it was practical and romantic. She knows me better than anyone else on earth, and I felt ready. So you put together her thinking and my feeling, and we have a green light!

I read and reread his profile several times. Each time it would sink in a little more that this guy (scarily) had everything I was looking for in a partner. And the bonus points kept racking up—he cooks, is handy around the house, accomplished in his profession, rugged, easygoing, spiritual, musical. Whewwww. I was beginning to think he might be the 'blender guy." You know girls, the one that has the best traits of every guy you've ever dated. With all the right ingredients (sweet, salty, tangy, cool, refreshing, intoxicating) to create the perfect margarita of a man. The butterflies were having a dance party, more like an orgy, and multiplying quickly. But I was still "on the wagon" from dating.

Physical Contact

I missed his first call, and I really don't like that first call to go to voicemail. Because then you hear his (nervous) voice before ever speaking to him and are faced with the apprehension of being the one to call back. I know I was the one who initiated the contact originally on Match by emailing him, and I am totally good with that. With Match, you have free reign in emailing people, winking at them, or waiting for them to contact you. I have no problem being bold in that context. I like to think I'm a bit old-fashioned, but my impatience back then took over and, to me, emailing him first was a bold move. But I still feel a guy should call the girl first. Tom told me that he liked when girls "winked" or emailed him on Match because it gave him the signal that there was interest in a medium that lacks eye contact or that flirty smile. It made me realize that guys are just looking for their "in" and then, believe me, if they have their act together and are confident in who they are, they will take it from there.

It took me all day to call him back. First, because I spent the day with my niece and nephews swimming and second, because, well, I was nervous. Remember the adrenaline pumping through my veins, sweating under my armpits, mouth as dry as the Sahara reaction with Portland? Yeah, that was happening again.

After 17 first dates, I still get nervous because I'm in this to find that very right person for me and each time I go on a date I'm thinking, okay, this could just be another guy, or this could be "the guy." Yeah, no pressure there. I'm an intense person and I put myself out there— heart on my sleeve, open, honest, with intention. And as you've discovered by now, I will leap. Leap right off the cliff with no parachute if I intuitively feel there's potential. I guess that makes me a huge risk-taker. But unlike betting on the stock market, I have a strong enough sense of self that mitigates risk, that even if my stock plummets and goes belly-up, I'm not going to lose the principal amount—I will always have the "me" I started with and the growing "interest" of some experience.

So I called Tom on my way back home into the city. Anyway, end result—he had a good voice, a really good voice, and that was all it took to get me excited again about a first date. And so our relationship commenced.

Did I mention he had a really, really good voice? It made me feel excited, calm, and curious, all at once. So good that as soon as I hung up with him, I called my sister-in-law and all I said was, "he has a good voice." That's all I needed to say because all of my girlfriends know what that means to me.

A man's voice, to me, can speak to not only your heart but also your soul. With every man, and I can attest to this after 18 first dates, I knew after speaking to each one on the phone, hearing his voice, if there would be something between us. So I smiled, big, because as soon as I heard his voice, I knew "something" was going to happen with me and this guy, a businessman, a musician, a bohemian San Francisco native.

Then I had to wait because he was heading out of town for the weekend. I am so impatient and being this excited and having to wait to even set up our date, let alone actually making it to the first date, was pure agony. Oh, and to torture myself even more, I had Googled him, found his Myspace account featuring his music and, Oh My God, his music was so awesome and beautiful. It touched my soul; it literally touched my soul. And quite frankly, I have an inner-groupie in me that becomes quite the swooner when faced with a tall, dark-haired handsome guy that can play the guitar and sing. And there were triple bonus points because he sang country music. I did grow up in Florida—loving country music is religion there. I never had a favorite rock idol growing up; I was always drawn to the talent, the intensity and, yes, for a while, the bad-boy edginess of musicians. Somewhere along the way, it transformed into the healthy swooning of businessmen who played guitar and sang! And I was totally swooning over this guy because I fell in love with his voice before we ever met in person. And did I mention I emailed a bunch of my girlfriends with tidbits of information about him (the "good voice") because I was so damn excited?!

He called just when he said he would so we could figure out our schedules. It was looking like our first date wouldn't happen until eight days after our first phone call. Come on girls, eight days, that might as well be a year. Okay, a little dramatic I agree, but seriously, I was very excited, and I could tell he was too. We had several short but connecting conversations. I don't remember exactly what happened, but I got an email from him saying that his schedule had opened up and he could meet a day earlier than we had planned. Oh yeah, I emailed him just to say hi and wish him a good time with a birthday date he had planned with his mom (yeah, how sweet is that, uhhh, heartstrings tugging). I was grinning from ear to ear on my way into my torturous exercise class after emailing him back saying, "Yes, let's do Thursday." After spending the week trying to just get to our Friday date, I was so darn excited it had been moved up to Thursday. And of course I was thinking, if it goes as well as I think it's going to, maybe we can go out Friday too. I sometimes wonder if men think ahead like this, but we do, don't we girls? China patterns picked out (in our heads) after that third amazing date. Our minds just go there, so easily, so quickly, and so dramatically.

It's All About the Ambiance

I met Tom for our first date at this cool, funky Asian restaurant a few blocks from Union Square in San Francisco. And as soon as we greeted each other, my nervousness subsided. The angst gave way to ease and joy for the moment. The restaurant had an air of romance and adventure powerful enough to sweep anyone off their feet with cozy, cushioned benches for intimate gatherings. Okay, I took that line directly from the restaurant's website. A bit hokey but a very accurate description. Since I already had one foot off the ground and still had butterflies in my stomach, I was swept pretty much immediately. And everything about the evening was absolutely everything a first date should be: fun, romantic, easy, exciting, promising…and a second date scheduled before the first one ends!

The conversation was effortless, the attraction was obvious, and the interaction relaxed. Here was a guy who was confident with himself and it showed in his presence with the situation. As I was to learn, he would always be my boy scout—always prepared, always organized, always ready with ideas and alternatives. Talk about feeling safe, comfortable, and cherished.

After dinner we went for an evening walk through the charming hidden cottage neighborhood with beautiful gardens along the Filbert Street steps. It is like walking into another time in some other country. Beautiful, quaint, seductive. And then there are the views—incredible skyline views of the city, the Bay Bridge, and the East Bay. I truly believe that just about any scenario can be romantic with the right person. But this, this was iconically romantic. Every girl should have a moment in their lives like this—the perfect background for a first kiss. After spending a little time completely in this beautiful moment full of sweetness and potential, Tom drove me home, walked me to my front door, and like the true gentleman that he is, kissed me goodnight and went home. Don't you love those kisses filled with tomorrow? That kiss left me filled with the anticipation of tomorrow and our next date. Smiley face :) Love that so much.

I will say this: all of my Match.com dates that morphed into some type of relationship started with a meal. Not a "meet and greet" but a mutual excitement and commitment to spend a little time together over a meal. I am serious about what I desire, and I am attracting men that have the same clarity. If I don't intuitively feel a connection or an excitement about someone, then meeting for coffee or a drink is truly just a time-filler.

I'm not looking for an easy out—I'm trusting myself and the Universe to bring men into my life who are worthy of my time and I of theirs. It's that simple.

Oh, the pure joy of reliving every moment of a great first date in our minds. I slept little and dreamt much. The next morning, I decided to email Tom to thank him for a great first date and flirtatiously see if he was interested in a second date that evening. I did this without provocation, without expectation, and with the complete openness that I really liked him and felt no reason to withhold those thoughts or feelings. I told you I leap. I don't play games or follow the myriad of dating rules. I follow my heart, I wear it on my sleeve, I speak up and out. If a guy can't handle it or isn't ready for it, well then, he isn't the right guy for me.

And Tom was just as excited as I was. He had no problem telling me that he wanted to see me the next night after our first date. He rearranged his plans for the evening and planned our second date. A drink then a movie, which led to dinner, then several options of which I chose good, old-fashioned necking in his car in not one, but several very romantic spots in San Francisco. Sorry girls, I'm keeping those locations to myself! What's so great about the tried and true movie night? Well, you get to cuddle in the theatre. No talking, just cuddling and hand-holding. So sweet. And what's so great about good, old-fashioned necking? Well, you only get it for that very short time in the very beginning of your relationship. So, enjoy it, relish in it, savor it. There are men who get that and they will appreciate it. Sex changes everything, it just does. So those first dates, the activities of the first encounters, are so precious. Kissing, cuddling, laughing, talking... pure intoxication.

Return of the Gentleman

Again my gentleman boy scout left me at my front door. Left me happy, grinning, and dreamily anticipating our third date planned for Sunday. As we parted very late on Friday evening, I was already so excited about our third date on Sunday morning. Tom had asked me on our first date if he could take me on a hike and picnic for our second date, which had become our third date. Are you following this? Picture one of those movie montages when people are falling for each other, and its snippet after snippet of romantic scenes with romantic background music. That is exactly what this looked and felt like.

I had really only been on a few other hikes in my entire life, so normally I would be a little nervous, but with Tom I felt completely comfortable in this adventure with him. What I didn't know was that our nature day would become one of the most memorable days of my existence.

Tom picked me up, and we headed north out of San Francisco to begin our day. We stopped at a gourmet grocery store in Sausalito to get food for our picnic. Cheeses and olives and crusty bread. And dates and salami and grapes. So much of so many favorites. All the essentials were already packed. My boy scout had a backpack with plates, utensils, cloth napkins (my favorite green color, green like spring grass), glasses, wine, a wine bottle opener, sunscreen, and blankets. He carried all of this and his guitar. Seriously girls—a tall, dark, handsome, prepared man carrying a guitar, a backpack picnic, wearing a plaid shirt and jeans leading you into nature—how damn sexy is that?! Oh, and by the way, he stopped along the hike to pick wildflowers for me: bright yellow California buttercups and sweet white popcorn flowers. Go ahead, be envious, put it in your mind, the intention that you want this experience too. As Martha Stewart would say, "It's a good thing." And I wish it for anyone and everyone who desires it.

The hike into the Marin Headlands was about forty minutes and placed us in the most astonishing piece of land overlooking Muir Beach. The sky was bright blue with wisps of fog grazing along the tops of the mountain. It was like sitting in heaven, above the Earth, certainly above civilization, floating in the fog with the golden haze of the sun warming the day.

Here's where the rest of the day becomes as wispy as the fog. I'm pretty sure the wine came first. And then food. And lots of conversation about families and the foundations of what became our lives. Maybe spirituality, maybe just chitchat. It must have been an intoxicating confluence of conversation and "stuff." Because, somewhere in there, the picnic became a naked picnic. Somewhere between the wine and the music and the chill of the fog came out a cozy plaid blanket to snuggle under. Which led to the heat of the moment turning into clothes flying out from under the blanket.

And nestled in those moments was kissing, but just kissing, and more wine, and grapes, and chocolate, and deep conversation, and laughter, and music. And the pure truth of knowing that this is part of a memory that will live with me forever. A pure spiritual truth, for me, of knowing I was exactly where I was supposed to be at that moment in time. Except I had no concept of time or any other existence except Tom and me naked on the side of a mountain. We were a part of the mountain and a part of nature, talking and laughing and him playing guitar and singing to me.

I was me—free-spirited, in the moment, content, and officially a "West Coast" girl. The remnants of my self-conscious East-Coastness drifted away with the fog leaving more "me" than had ever existed before this day. I could have stayed on that mountain forever. Okay, well, not really. I was at the beginning of thinking I needed to pee and was not too keen on squatting behind a bush. Naked on a mountain fine…peeing behind a bush, not so much.

We reluctantly left our perfect day for the reality of responsibility. Tom needed to prepare for a very important meeting the next day, and even though I was a little disappointed about this, I really did understand the importance for his career and wanted to be supportive. I was disappointed though; I tend to get distracted by romance and have to shepherd myself back to responsibility. I remember wanting a little more time, a little more Tom.

If this were one of those fluffy romance novels, the picnic would have never ended, there would have been no impromptu bodily functions to tend to, and certainly real life would not have intervened. And so, in the world of courtship, our amazing third date ended.

And our fourth date was only 24 hours away. Tom wanted to cook dinner for me, and we decided to do this at my house because he actually hadn't been inside my apartment yet. A few phone calls and a busy workday for Tom later, he arrived at my apartment with two bags of groceries and another great bottle of wine. Let me tell you, as sexy as a tall, dark, handsome man carrying a picnic and a guitar, and wearing a plaid shirt and jeans is...a tall, dark, handsome man cooking you a meal from scratch in your kitchen—we're way off the sexy chart here. I just remember sitting in my comfy woven seagrass chair that is in the sunny nook in my kitchen, drinking a glass of wine, watching this man cook me dinner, chatting about the day, and I seriously couldn't imagine anything more perfect, more sweetly domestic, more right.

We ate dinner over candlelight, sitting at my bistro table that sits in front of my bay window overlooking 24th Street. Chatting, drinking wine, enjoying this wonderful meal that Tom prepared. I know girls, you want to hear about the "desert." The juicy details about sex. Because you're thinking this is so awesome, so amazing, so romantic. A deliberate and enchanting courtship...almost perfect. Almost perfect.

Here's the thing: even though we were quite attracted to each other, the chemistry was...just...off. Ouch. I think that many of you can relate, yes? Those great men who show up in our lives who we are so excited about but...for one, or both of you, that illustrious chemistry of physical, romantic attraction is not only not hot, it's like tepid bathwater that's been sitting too long. Ummm, like you had the tub filling up with yummy hot water, you added the bubbles, lit the candles, turned on your favorite music, and then got a phone call from your mother! And by the time you got back to your perfect bath, it had gone from sexy to steamed out and a bit sterile. The question is, do you take a step in because you've invested in the setup, or do you pull the plug, blow out the candles and turn the music off?

A Gentleman Never Lies

Three days later we had our fifth and final date. We sat across the table from each other in a funky, casual Yucatan restaurant down the street from my apartment. I already knew what was going to happen. My damn intuition is always right, and well, Tom met me at the restaurant, (his idea) instead of coming to my door to get me, and I just knew. And Tom, so sweet and honest, sat across from me and said, "Our chemistry is off." It was important for him to have an electric connection and chemistry with the women he was dating, and I'm so glad he was willing to be honest about that. And to be honest that he didn't feel that with me.

I think I laughed because I knew it. We talked about how is it possible that two people who liked each other so much, were so attracted to each other, and so compatible could be missing this very vital thing to turn a romance into a love story?! Okay, well, we didn't talk about that last bit, but I was certainly thinking that part. Ughhhhhhhhhhh. We talked about being friends. And we both knew it was the right and only thing to do, but it still hurt.

This man who had come into my life as the perfectly blended margarita had left me with the hangover of cheap tequila. Numb, dizzy, queasy. Okay, I'm being dramatic again. My point here is that there is no "cooking time" for how long a person has to be in the oven of your life to leave a mark. This man had left an indelible mark of only sweet memories of being courted and romanced in some of my favorite old-fashioned ways. Okay, the naked picnic may not be old-fashioned, but it was just so darn fun and spontaneous!

During our time together, Tom and I talked about a YouTube video he wanted to make for one of the songs on his CD that he recorded the prior year. It was my favorite song and the general population's favorite as well. The song challenges the audience to produce a legacy that is more than material goods. I offered my unsolicited feedback as to what it meant for me. However, just a few days after Tom and I stopped seeing each other, that conversation and that song would inspire me to do so much more. And that is truly the impetus for writing this book.

And so, in the pause of a beautiful courtship, this man, a businessman, a musician, a bohemian San Francisco native, my boy scout wrapped in a flannel shirt and a guitar left me with the gift of romance, honesty, and inspiration.

My Invitation to You

*B*eyond the List. Here's the thing: having your list and knowing your priorities are incredibly valuable. Trusting your body's awareness is priceless. For the times someone has checked all the boxes on your list but you or they weren't attracted to your body and one of you ended things, be grateful, be very grateful. We're talking about romantic dating and partnership here, and if a long-term or lifelong partnership is something you seek, please add this to your list: there must be a mutual admiration and appreciation of each other as well as mutual affection, attraction, and adoring of each other's bodies.

I'm not talking about mind-blowing, can't breathe without him attraction; that has its own pitfalls. I'm talking about innate affection, caring, and yummy attraction to his home (his body). Meeting someone and expecting them to change or that you'll grow into liking their bodies more is not a kindness to them or you. Everyone deserves to be appreciated, admired, and adored by their lover - spouse for exactly who they are. And not having that oftentimes creates a disparate and disintegrating romantic partnership reduced to feeling like trapped roommates. The yum is possible; let your body give you information.

> *I admire, applaud, and appreciate your courage,*
> *XO, Danna*

---

* *Do you desire space to reflect and journal? Visit the "Invitation to Go Deeper" section at the end of the book.*

"I love you not only for who you are, but for what you are when I am with you. I love you not only for what you have made of yourself, but what you are making of me."

~Roy Croft

Chapter 11

Regifting: The Gift of Contribution

The Golden Gate Bridge is symbolic to the world and especially symbolic to me. It symbolizes San Francisco to many—the end of one journey and the beginning of another for me. It's a landmark. An icon. It is a massive structure of strength and grace. It "disappears" when the fog rolls in and wraps itself around it. But you know it's there. You always know it's there. Like your own knowing. Like the Universe having your back. Sometimes you can physically see, or hear, these things—in nature, in music, in people, in yourself. And sometimes they are invisible, but you still know that they are there. And when you perceive them, you feel their power in your heart, your spirit, your being. That is what happens to me each and every time I drive back into San Francisco from Marin. Each and every time I catch that first glimpse of the Golden Gate, I feel its power, in my heart, in my being, and in my spirit. It reminds me of the place where my spirit resonates and lives joyously... of my own glorious journey.

And our journeys can be great gifts to others in ways we can't even imagine. As you know, the song that was written by my amazing guy wrapped in a flannel shirt and a guitar inspired me to begin to know my legacy. That's what the song was about, that's the call to action that began welling up within me, to discover and live my legacy, no matter what it was. Many years later, I was reading an interview with Hoda Kotb, a broadcast journalist and the main co-anchor of the NBC morning show *Today*, about a story of her taking an undesired but necessary plane trip during her cancer treatments. While talking to the passenger seated beside her, she chose vulnerability, and she chose to share some of her story. But at the end of the flight, she paused and said that she hoped her row mate would remember her for more than this intermittent story, her cancer, that it's not what she wanted people to think about. And he responded by telling her not to rob people of her journey, for there is great vulnerability, connection and inspiration there.

For much of my life, I have kept my greatest journey secret from the world and from myself. First it was to separate the good from the bad, the right from the wrong. I was trying to live without acknowledging all the healing work it had taken in the process of trying to create my life. Then it was to separate the success from the shame. Like a celebrity's child who wants to make it big on their own laurels instead of embracing their entire experience of who they are and how that has actually influenced who they have become. The influences, the threads of our journey, become just the words that someone else needs to hear to continue to weave their life together or have the courage to change the fabric of the life they've been living.

If we don't look within, if we don't choose courageous kindness, and if we don't change the conversation we are having not only with ourselves but with others about the men in our lives, are we not robbing ourselves and the world of vulnerability, connection, and inspiration?

Making Lemons Into Lemonade

If you're reading this, I know you are choosing something different. I know you are seeking more consciousness, more awareness, more delicious possibilities. I also know it's not always easy peasy lemon squeezy; it just isn't. Choosing to be more present and living from our authentic being is a process and a practice. We stumble, we are challenged, and sometimes we are bitch-slapped by the Universe. But we are choosing, and that is a powerful thing—YOUR choice is powerful. I hope you get that. I hope by the end of this book you get that so much more! Taking the time to acknowledge new and different choices, the little shifts and changes along the way, that tells the Universe, "hey, yeah, I get it, I see it, I feel ya having my back, let's keep going!"

I purchased Wayne Dyer's book *The Power of Intention* many years ago for Pat, my ex-husband. It sat on the shelf for years, then got packed away, shipped

3,000 miles to San Francisco, unpacked, placed in the bookshelf of my new apartment, and finally opened. But I believe that just by having the book in my possession long before I cracked it open, long before I looked at a single page, and long before I read the first word, I was moving intentionally. Intentionally forward to a place where I could give back.

Opening that book and reading the pages provided me with even more direction and even more framework for a life I had already begun to live intentionally. His philosophy was that if you change the way you look at things, the things you look at will change. I see what my choices are creating. I know I am leaving evidence of my choices, creating the life I desire; the evidence is woven throughout my life.

Creativity

I sit in my living room in my charming Noe Valley, San Francisco flat. I look around the room. I see my interior design talent and passions in full view, on every surface. What once was a blank canvas of white walls and empty rooms is now filled with color, warmth, and life. One-third of my possessions from my house in Tampa have taken up residence in this apartment. One-third of my possessions and 100% of my creativity have turned this house into a home.

Kindness

Once a month, on a Friday morning, I join my two pastors at Grupo de la Comida Food Bank at a church in the Mission District of San Francisco. This is where organizers and volunteers come together with homeless and impoverished people to share food. You see, once a month the government delivers cases of canned goods, maybe jars of peanut butter or containers of orange juice. Along with the USDA food delivery, there are bushels of fresh produce, bread, grains, and rice. And together with a few dozen volunteers, we organize the food and distribute it to the hundreds of people who have wrapped themselves in a line around the church. In this act of volunteerism, I am participating in a greater act, that of kindness toward others, and kindness toward myself because I receive so much joy in participating in this simple act of handing cans of food to total strangers.

Love

My niece and I share special girl-time sleepovers. Each time we have a sleepover, I try to find something different for us to do together. From playing in the little park on 24th and Douglass Streets, to experiencing the butterfly garden at The Flower Conservatory in Golden Gate Park, to driving by the famous Painted Ladies in Alamo Square or dipping our toes in the Pacific at Ocean Beach.

And each time we are together, I make it my mission to point out the amazing things we see during our time together. I point out The Golden Gate Bridge as it first comes into sight on our way south into the city from Marin. I point out the fog as it rolls along the mountain tops. I point out the view of downtown and the splendor of the tall buildings.

And together we choose the simple things. Chocolate milk or hot chocolate from Starbucks. Which flavor of gelato to eat for dessert (we have decided there should be a pickle flavor). And my favorite: which flower smells the best at the Noe Valley Flower Shop. That day, we smelled every single flower and finally agreed on the white tuberose, although the pink peony was a close second.

It is in my love for my niece that I want to share my love for the simple things in life. And in watching her wonderment and joy in these simple things, I feel love in return. It really is so true that there's as much joy in giving a gift as receiving one. Each time I created an experience was like giving a gift in watching her interact and respond as only kids can, with their truest selves.

Beauty

As I sit in the nook in my kitchen where my desk resides in front of the window, I look to the west and see the fog gently rolling in over the mountains, down to my valley, across the rooftops, and I am reminded of the awe-inspiring beauty that exists just outside my window. And because of my journey and my grace in acknowledging the gifts I have been given, I am reminded of the awe-inspiring beauty that now resides within me. While I may not take in every moment with gratitude, or stop to smell every flower and bask in its beauty and scent, I do, often, pause throughout my day, throughout my moments, and nod to the Universe. Those pauses, those nods, have silently etched the song of beauty within me. No one can take it away, nothing can erase it; it is etched in residence where I can linger and loiter anytime I choose.

Expansion

I see the beautifully, hand-carved wooden box where Harley's (my deceased dog) things now reside. His ashes, his sweater from when we lived in New York City, his toothbrush, the collars he received each Christmas, numerous sympathy cards from his passing, the plaster paw print the doctors and nurses at the animal hospital made that day, and other odds and ends that simply are Harley.

But that box is also filled with creativity, kindness, love, and beauty. In all the acts of people who helped take care of Harley during his illness. In all the acts of compassion that came after Harley's passing.

But I look again, and I see all that has occurred since that day. Every action I have taken to move forward, to be able to stand in my apartment in San Francisco, and I recognize that every single one of those actions was an act of expansion that created and continue to create the life I dream. It is our choices that galvanize into a million little things constantly creating our existence. We may not want to know that, we may not want to have that responsibility for ourselves, but the sooner and faster we own it, the sooner and faster we can explode into possibility and implode our limitations.

Abundance

As I stand outside, I look out to my future. I look up to the sky to silently thank the Universe, and I see my favorite time of day right before dusk turns to night…indigo sky. It's my favorite time of day because it's as if the Earth stands still for a moment to pause, to silently nod to the Universe for the collaboration in completing another perfect day. It is when I look into the vastness of the indigo sky that I see the unlimited abundance of the Universe. And I know from experience that it is my choice.

My choice to choose happiness, my choice to choose creativity, my choice to choose kindness, my choice to choose love. And in choosing these things, I am choosing to participate in a Universe of abundance. And the Universe has given me unlimited abundance in the gifts of presence, hope, wisdom, intention, self, freedom, forgiveness, excitement, encouragement, harmony, passion, music, healing, clarity, adventure, friendship, romance, honesty, and inspiration. All the gifts I received through my men, all the gifts I received through empowering myself.

Receptivity

Gift-giving requires at least two people. It requires one person to give the gift, and it requires one person to receive the gift. I ponder all the gifts that were given to me by these amazing men, and I realize that in order to truly be given those gifts, I had to be willing to receive them. And I am humbled that the Universe has provided me with that grace.

I'm so curious what you and the Universe are cooking up as the legacy you'll leave in this world. How much fun can you have collaborating together, aligned with your priorities, feeding and nurturing them into existence? And the men you've dated, been dating, are dating or the one that you're living with, creating a life with—are they, is he, included in the grace and gratitude of your intentions?

Will you show your sisters, daughters, and nieces the admiration, adoration, and appreciation that is possible with and for men? Or, will you leave the world with criticisms and complaints about your men, filling the air like secondhand smoke? In each choice, we are either nurturing our desires or sabotaging them; filtering energies out into our sphere of influence. These gifts, these gifts we've been pondering and receiving, are you willing to let them out and into the hearts of your world as the regift of contribution?

My Invitation to You

Start an "acknowledgment of you" list! I use my iPhone. And as I sift through my days, I jot down different choices and actions that are generating and engaging me in authentic ways. Some of my current acknowledgments include finding a book cover designer; submitting a proposal to speak at a women's organization; reaching out to someone I know through social media to meet for coffee; walking to the farmers' market for groceries; deleting a dating app that isn't feeling good; saying yes to the man I met in the grocery store. You get the idea. There are no rules except to not judge yourself for what you did or didn't do.

Start an "acknowledgment of him" list! Living intentionally includes acknowledging the energies and actions your guy is choosing that also feed your desires. He spent ten extra minutes in bed snuggling with you. He called your mom with you and chatted. He walked to the farmers' market with you and you shopped together.

You get the idea. There are no rules except to not judge him for what he did or didn't do.

I admire, applaud, and appreciate your courage,
XO, Danna

---

* *Do you desire space to reflect and journal? Visit the "Invitation to Go Deeper" section at the end of the book.*

"And you, a windrose, a compass, my direction, my description of the world."
~Ian Burgham

Chapter 12

Dessert: The Gift of 'Big Love' AKA Choice, Awareness, and Infinite Possibilities

*M*y friend, life coach, and pastor (yes, this is one person, one beautiful person) recently sent me this note after one of my aforementioned heartaches:

"In the book The Last Lecture Randy Pausch says that there are often walls placed right before our dreams because he thinks it forces us to show ourselves just how much we want something. If we're willing to fight to get over that last wall.

Perhaps you are standing at one of those walls? You are so close to so many dreams ... I can see them. Stay focused on what you ultimately want and as we take each step closer, sometimes with tears in our eyes, we will summit the wall. I promise."

As I talk about each of the amazing men I have unwrapped for you, I also recognize the pain and grace it took to acknowledge the gifts each have given me. And it is in that grace that I continue to climb the wall. Because just on the other side, I firmly know I will have and will be more of who I am, while also continuing to have beautiful collaborations and a lifelong romantic partnership.

My 'San Francisco'

How will I know him? He will have the traits, attributes, and qualities that I desire and require in a partner. He will be accessible, responsive, and engaged with creating loving kindness, unconditional giving, respect, friendship, encouragement, the ability to negotiate differences, commitment, interdependence, teamwork, compatibility (common interests and an appreciation of our differences), harmony (the ease and enjoyment of moving through the day with each other), and chemistry (bodies that actively pull to one another, seek each other out in comfort and desire).

Simply, the One (for me) will be my San Francisco—he will take my breath away and allow me to breathe deeply and enjoy life just by being himself.

And how do I continue to envision this dream for my future? I go to my "happy place." I drive up and over the hills of San Francisco, north across the majestic Golden Gate Bridge, through the mountains and the suburbs, to the countryside where cows and horses roam alongside rustic farmhouses, fragrant vineyards, and chic wineries to the oldest square in America: Sonoma Square.

I have been visiting Sonoma Square since I was a teenager. I walk around the square and visit the shops, I go to the little deli and indulge in the decadence of a prosciutto and brie sandwich, then I walk across the street to the park in the middle of the square. I sit in the midst of nature, in the soft, green grass, surrounded by brightly colored flowers, sheltered under the canopy of trees, with the duck pond just in sight. I inhale the nature. I inhale the scenery. I inhale my future.

Because each and every time I marvel at the unchanged phenomenon—families picnicking, children playing, and dogs romping. It is a frozen moment in time. A moment in time that definitively overflows my cup with sheer bliss and anticipation and with absolute clarity of the life that I am creating.

I realize it's not that there is one right person, one soul mate, one true love. I realize there are many right persons, many soul mates, and many true loves that walk with us for a while during our journey. Some longer than others, some with tragic endings, some with no endings—the ones that we can reintegrate into our lives in another way. Or maybe they were never a lover but still felt like a right one, soul mate, true love and the physical existence of that knowing never materialized into a physical relationship but still…they were a soul mate. They were someone with whom you had a strong affinity, an unexplainable connection generating lessons and experiences so deep and profoundly life-affirming or, perhaps, life-altering.

The concept of one right person, one soul mate, one true love is fatally romantic and fatally flawed. The flaw exists in the scarcity that surrounds it. In a world where the Universe is friendly and loving and kind, how could there be just one right person for each person in a world with billions of amazing people? In a world where every two people that connect have their own unique dynamic. The perfection exists in the abundance that expands our hearts when we know and believe this. I look back and smile, thinking about all the amazing men I've acknowledged here because I know that any one of them could have been "The One." There was a space of possibility with each them or we never would have met and gone out and explored each other. The entire Universe conspires to bring people into our lives to give us endless choices. We have the honor of making choices to create awareness and possibilities for our future. How freakin' cool is that?! I chose each of those experiences, one for years, and another for months, and yet another for a few weeks. And so it goes that each of them, each of my amazing men, was the absolute right person for me at that time ... for a time that was undisclosed when we began.

Coveting Carrot Cake

And yet still I dream of something bigger, something like the Fleur de Sel cupcake at my very favorite, obsessively ridiculously chic cupcake store around the corner from my house. Fleur de Sel cupcakes are the richest chocolate with an over-the-top sweetness of caramel sprinkled with the decadence of course sea salt. I dream of these cupcakes just like I dream of that big love. A friend told me once that's because that is who I am with my men: big love, big, juicy, affectionate, adoring, open to the possibilities of love. That's actually how I am with a lot of my life, and I continue to ask for that everywhere, especially with myself.

I desire the "something bigger." The spark of a new recipe in my mind to cook for that special man, the thing that steals a glow across my face in the middle of a business meeting because of him, the thing that takes my breath away when I get a glimpse of him coming around the corner, and the thing that gives me pause to inhale so deeply when that same man holds me close and I breathe him into every cell of my being.

I cherish this possibility of something bigger with as much delight as I cherish my favorite chocolate cupcakes. And yet I also covet something else, something even greater. Carrot cake. Yes, carrot cake. I covet the carrot cake of men and partnership because carrot cake has substance that is still with you when you wake up in the morning. It fills your senses, and it satisfies your sweet tooth while rather overtly feeding you nutrients (carrots, raisins, nuts).

What do you cherish? What do you covet?

Will you step into the bakery and delight your senses, tickle your fancy, and allow the Universe to sprinkle your life with the bittersweet memories that invite you to the divinity of your carrot cake?

My Invitation to You

*H*ow many of you only go into the bakery to look, refusing to indulge and enjoy what your heart desires? How many of you will only eat gluten-free bread or no bread at all when your body is screaming for that carrot cake? I challenge you to look at some of the rules you have chosen, and play with what your choices create when you choose from them and when you choose from joy, from what lights you up. Notice. Just notice. And, please, oh please, a tiny bit more, choose what you cherish and covet and enjoy the f@ck out of the possibilities those choices create.

I admire, applaud, and appreciate your courage,
XO, Danna

---

* *Do you desire space to reflect and journal? Visit the "Invitation to Go Deeper" section at the end of the book.*

"Consciousness is the most elegant force for change in the world."
~Dr. Dain Heer

Chapter 13
Afterglow

At two a.m. in the middle of my cozy bed, I was awakened by a shake, whale songs swirling through the air from my computer, and the shadows from the street lights dancing through the windows. While my sleep-fogged brain was attempting to register if there was an earthquake, I took inventory. My heart was pounding; I was alone as I had been for the last six months, still feeling the tiniest of tugs at my heart to open my eyes and not see My Love sleeping next to me. The bed was not rolling or shaking, the room was still, no earthquake. Safe. I took a deep breath, and the Universe leaned in and whispered in my ear, "Let's talk."

What are you going to do when the Universe stirs your soul awake from a deep sleep asking to engage with you, asking for your presence, insisting now is the time? More frequently than not, I am learning to oblige. If the Universe is willing to have my back 24/7 without any qualms about time, resources, or convenience, I was surely willing to meet it exactly when and where I was asked. And so, the pillow talk ensued.

Category 5!

"I'm filling up, there's not much room left," said the Universe. "Please say more," I asked, "I thought you were infinite, what's the problem?" Images of television shows, movies, social media, and women chatting flashed through my head like lightning strikes …

"Men are scum."

"Men are dicks and assholes."

"Men are lazy and stupid."

"If you want something done right, don't ask a man, do it yourself."

"I don't need anything from a man."

"I hate men, I wish they would all disappear."

"The future is female."

The lightning strikes climaxed into roars of thunder as they battered silently against the hearts of half the population on earth.

Then fragments of conversations I had seen, heard, or had with men whirled about my head like a tornado picking up priceless possessions only to redisburse them in a pile of debris.

"What did I do to deserve being called scum?"

"I certainly have a dick, and it was once coveted as part of the priceless commodity of reproduction of the human race. That's not relevant anymore?!"

"What part of not having the knowledge of something yet or not jumping to engage in something at someone else's desire makes me stupid and lazy?"

"Sure, I've had my moments of being an asshole, who hasn't? But it doesn't make me an all-encompassing generalization, does it?!"

"Women don't need me, literally for anything, and they tell me with such vileness, it's like I'm just wrong for existing and being alive as a man."

"If the future is female, do I become extinct?"

Eye of the Storm

The flashes, whirling, and thundering subsided, stillness and silence filling the room with an eerie sense of peace that reminded me of growing up in Florida and bearing witness to being smack in the middle of the eye of a hurricane. The Universe, weary from the battle and teary-eyed from the heartbreaking cacophony of events, looked at me and said, "These words and actions are creating an energetic storm so catastrophic that I'm being filled up with the sooty refuse of judgment. Little can exist in this space of judgment. Survival takes over and the possibility of thriving as a collaborative species collapses."

"Truth," I said, "what will it take to turn this problem into the possibility of a thriving existence between men and women?" "Dare," said the Universe, "judgment cannot exist in the space of gratitude. Are you willing to be a voice of that different possibility?"

The definition of insanity from Albert Einstein is doing the same thing over and over again and expecting a different result. If you are a woman who has uttered any of the phrases above, or something similar, I'm daring you to change the conversation. I get it. I'm one of those women. Did you think that I'm sitting pretty as someone who is always a positive Pollyanna? I've full-on said many of the comments mentioned above and, maybe even worse, sat by and listened to others making those comments without speaking up.

Let's get real ladies, absolutely, without a doubt, there are moments we're upset and angry. There are moments we are truly physically protecting ourselves. You don't need me to tell you to do and say whatever it takes to protect yourself from physical harm. But what I want to say is that the words spoken in vain, frustration, anger, resentment, and even snippy sarcasm, they reverberate out into the world at an alarming speed and force. They have an impact. They create collateral damage.

From Wikipedia: "collateral damage is any death, injury, or other damage inflicted that is an unintended result of military operations." When we are treating the other sex like the opposite sex, we are in opposition to them. And like war, we are treating them like adversaries rather than allies. I think of divorce and breakups, oftentimes as a love that has turned into a war. I think of a relationship I was in for four years where the ex-wife criticized, belittled, and blamed my partner at the time for every possible thing, much of it in front of their son. In person, over the phone, and behind our backs. The mother and child would speak on speakerphone when he was at our house, and I would hear her say, "your dad isn't doing it right, tell him this…" or "tell your dad to pay for this, he should…" (even though he was paying more than required in child support). She would also tell the child, "I love your dad and always will."

How confusing is that?! That boy will grow up with the message that men are incompetent. He has experienced his father being emasculated in front of him, and he has been taught that love is inclusive of man-hating. That boy will someday be a man influenced by these ongoing experiences. That is collateral damage.

I told you early on in this book that I too have found myself at times doing these things. And it scared me, it shamed me and suffocated my sweet, loving nature to "change or die." I have felt emotional dying and have witnessed what could have been physical death. And I have witnessed in myself and others the presence and resilience to move forward with and from the choices of vibrant, kind empowerment of self. Leading from that elegant force of consciousness will always create something greater in your life and the world.

So like I said, I dare you, no, double-dog dare you to be the one to start changing the conversation. To own your words and responses. To give up resisting and reacting to or aligning and agreeing with an invented construct that we are at war with men. Isn't there another way to fit in, if that's important to you? Isn't there another way to be the strength and power you want to be? Isn't there another way to shift the struggle?

The Wind Whisperer

A friend of mine who lives about twenty-five minutes north of me in the town of San Rafael recently shared a story of finding herself, her family, and her home in the eye of a hurricane, so to speak, when a brush fire took light on the hills around her house. The entire neighborhood was gathered, all intently focused on the flames. "Oh my God, there's so much fire!" "Oh my God, it's coming this way!" "Holy shit, it's going to burn the neighborhood down!" My friend watched as, with each comment, the space between the flames grew smaller and the fire grew larger, engulfing more land. It was as if the fire was taking direct orders from the collective conversation of something more powerful than it ... the judgment of and from the people.

"Is that possible?" My friend wondered. The potential disaster seemingly imminent, my friend looked around, feeling the tug of the wind. She looked around at her family and said, "Hey, is it possible that the fire is reacting to the judgments and points of view being impelled at it from the people? Can you feel the wind tugging at us? I wonder what it knows?

"Hey there, magnificent wind, you sure are strong and powerful. You're like a bear hug from the Universe! I wonder though if you could move, just a bit over to the left? Could you do that for us? We would still feel your strapping strength, and you would also be providing us with safety for our families and our homes." The family asked again for a different possibility than what seemed inevitable.

Their energy was soft and sincere. Their vulnerability potent enough to power a city. And the wind with its own strength capable of powering a city with its unwavering force ... shifted ... a bit over to the left. My friend and her family had just changed a conversation that created the space for something else to become available.

Fault Line

So, at two a.m., in the middle of my cozy bed, I was awakened by a shake, whale songs swirling through the air from my computer and the shadows from the street lights dancing through the windows. The bed was not rolling or shaking, the room was still, no earthquake. Safe. I took a deep breath, and the Universe leaned in and whispered in my ear, "Thank you."

Ladies, you have the power. You have the vulnerability, softness, sincerity, and strength to change this conversation. Let me be the first one to lean in and whisper in your ear ..."*Thank you.*"

My Invitation to You

*L*et's Change the conversation! I was recently on a
walk at Chrissy Field along the beach and while
talking with a group of women, all in their 50s and 60s
I had just met, this transpired: One of the women was
telling the story about a harbor seal she had seen floating
in the water with his flipper outstretched, waiting for the
nearby fishermen on the pier to throw him bait to eat.
Another of the women remarked, "He's a lazy one, just
like all men." Whoa! I was floored, how do you go from
telling a cute story about a harbor seal to lambasting all
men in one fell swoop?! I was speechless and, for several
reasons, did not respond. One, I had just met these people,
and I suppose I didn't want to confront or affront anyone.
And two, I'm not very quick on my feet and couldn't
think of anything to say in a gracious, succinct, and inviting (of another possibility) way. Let's just say this was on
my mind, and in my heart, so much that I did come up
with some things I could have said. SO, ladies, what if we
use our strength, vulnerability, and power to change the
conversation and perhaps say this, not that ...

•   "All men are lazy."

- Oh gosh, I'm sorry you've had that experience with *All* men. I know so many hardworking, industrious, creative, (fill in the blank) men.
- "Men are idiots and can't do anything right."
  - I know so many brilliant and smart men. I admire their thinking and have come to realize more and more that just because they do something maybe totally different than I would, it's just different, not wrong. And my way isn't necessarily right, just different. I'm really learning to appreciate how our brains may just be different!
- "I don't need a man or any men."
  - That's such an interesting comment to me. For me, personally, with the leadership work I've been doing, I have found that the more I'm open to receiving from everyone, men and women, the more gratitude I have, the greater my life becomes, and the more enjoyable everyone is.
- "Men are scum, dicks, assholes, etc."
  - Can we take that down a level? We all know how horrible it feels and incorrect it is when we are grouped and lumped together as collective (unkind/untrue) generalizations. What else is possible?

I admire, applaud, and appreciate your courage,
XO, Danna

★ *Do you desire space to reflect and journal? Visit the "Invitation to Go Deeper" section at the end of the book.*

"Gratitude is not only the greatest of virtues, but the parent of all others."

~Cicero

Chapter 14

The Thank You Note: The Gift of Gratitude

Each night at ten p.m., my cell phone task reminder alarm goes off. The task reminder simply says, "Three Good Things." It is my daily reminder to take a moment to identify and appreciate three good things that I experienced during the day. So many days I have been blessed with many more than three things. During the more challenging times, those past few years, I would actually write down my moments of appreciation. Today I simply, and silently, announce them to myself. Then I simply, and silently, thank God and the Universe for the abundance of my "Three Good Things."

There are the short and sweet "Three Good Things" like the Mint Mojito Iced Coffee from Philz. A great night's sleep. Or the afternoon hike at Rodeo Beach in Sausalito. Oh, and turning off all social media, phone, and computer and snuggling into a good movie, buttered popcorn, and my guy. Or the joy of a new client saying yes to themselves and to me with my services. You get the idea. They could go unnoticed or unacknowledged, or you can acknowledge them with gratitude and continue to ask for more. I used to think that was being greedy, and now I know it's being gracious and generous with myself and with the world.

There's also the bigger, more impactful "Three Good Things" of people, places, and things that I am thankful for. So many people have not only witnessed my journey but have traveled with me, for a time, along my path. Some were landmarks to guide me through dark or confusing crossroads like the last year with my ex-husband, or Chapter 6's "Wrapped in Cargo Shorts and a Hawaiian Shirt" as you've come to know him. Some were stepping stones to move me forward along precarious ground, like my life coach mentioned in Chapter 9, and let's not forget Chapter 9's "Wrapped in Sneakers and a Cup of Tea." He was very much a part of my "Three Good Things" with his friendship, adventure, and clarity.

Some were bridges that helped me to walk over seemingly impassable obstacles, like my dear, dear friend Bob, who passed away soon after I moved to San Francisco. His life and spirit assisted me in finding the gift of perspective and wisdom in Chapter 4. Dear, bold, brilliant Mr. Ray, you are loved and missed and so appreciated. And all were voices of cheer, encouragement, and direction. Through sharing, participating, and for some, in just being. Whether in physical actions and voices or in me silently observing their own journeys to learn the lessons I needed to travel just a bit further.

When did I take this first step, this first step of thousands to get me physically and spiritually to exactly where I am today—writing my story, writing to potential employers, writing to my potential Mr. Right in the form of exchanging emails on Match.com and looking forward to meeting that last first date. That is such a philosophical question with such an existential answer. But what I do know resolutely is that I have always had love and support along the way.

Closing the Gap

My friend Lynne was with me the day I boarded the plane with my cat Lucy to fly the 3,000 miles from Tampa to San Francisco to begin this new journey in my life. Originally, we talked about driving the 3,000 miles. Pulling a little "Thelma and Louise" adventure across the country to initiate the start of my new life; stopping in various cities along the way to enjoy food, fun, and environment. However, finances and our forty-something bodies (and brains) decided it was more prudent to take the eight-hour plane flight versus the week and a half long car drive to get me to my new home and to start the process of getting me settled in. I remember Lynne and I sitting on the plane with Lucy, my cat, between us on the seat. We looked at each other, somewhere over Arizona I think, and laughed. We laughed because after only six hours on the plane, we were so ready to be in San Francisco and so damn glad we had chosen a much more efficient means of transportation.

Not only did Lynne fly with me to San Francisco, but she stayed with me for two weeks, sleeping on an air mattress in my empty apartment. She was a cleaning freak. And I was an organization freak. And we had a third person with us who was an analytical freak. We were this machine of cleaning, organizing, and analyzing how to make a 100-year-old apartment work for a woman who was used to the modern upgrades of a new house. Let me tell you, in two weeks my apartment was scrubbed from top to bottom, painted from top to bottom, and modernized (as much as possible) from top to bottom. And every box was unpacked, broken down, and dispensed of before my guests left. True supporters of physically settling me into my new home. For that, I will always be so grateful. Not just because of the physical effort exerted, but because of the teamwork and encouragement that took place at such a pivotal space in time for me.

Return Visit

Being able to seemingly go back to a space in time is also such a gracious act. I had the opportunity to do this after only two months in my new home. My former employer flew me down to Tampa to do some consulting work, allowing me to step back into the stream of my former life and to experience some of my favorite things, especially some of my favorite "Danna Day" things. I stayed with Cindy's family for my entire visit, so I actually got eleven days of family time, and it was so physically and emotionally nurturing for me. To be able to wake up and eat breakfast with the kids, to have movie time, to eat dinner with the family, to devour Cindy's baking phenomenons, and to just be in something so familiar.

During that time, I also got to visit with my other close friends, share meals with them, share story-time with their kids, share my journey with them, and relish in their company. The same holds true for being able to spend time with my former employees. A lot can happen in just two months—babies are born, new jobs are started, and a lot stays the same. It was fun to catch up on the new and to notice the familiar.

Being in someplace so familiar and experiencing something so completely serendipitous also occurred. One of my favorite things to do on "Danna Day" was to go to The First Unity Church in St. Petersburg, and I was so happy that I would be able to attend services during my trip back to Tampa. Not only did I get to attend services, but I got to attend services with my Tampa life coach, which had so much meaning for me to sit next to this woman who had taught me so much and who had been such a vital part of me taking those first decisive, courageous steps into my new life.

I remember sitting in the pew next to Dianne, in the pews I had sat in so many times before. But this time was different because I had two months of a new life sitting with me in that pew. Two months of complete newness sitting with me in the oldness of the church I had been to so many times. New things and people like my apartment, "Portland" (whom I was dating at the time), using my feet as transportation, new friends, weekly dinners with family, all things that did not exist in my life just two short months earlier.

Who else knows this? Knows what it's like to experience a complete shift in your reality so quickly? Have you ever moved to a new city? Raise your hand, because you know what I'm talking about. Have you had a baby? Raise your hand, because you know exactly what I'm talking about and could teach the rest of us a thing or two about total reality shifts. Have you had someone close to you die? Moved in with someone? Gotten married? Traveled to another country? Started a new job? I can feel the hands raised. Sometimes we get, well, a little or a lot stuck in the now of impatience of wanting something different than where we are, what we are, or what we have. Yeah, I have both hands raised right now. And I can lower them into a thankful prayer pose because through these gifts I unequivocally know how instantaneously life can transform. I'm more peaceful now in the now, and when I tap into three months out and look back, I can smile mischievously with ravenous delight and stubborn surrender.

Joyfully Ever After

And as I finish this chapter of my life, a decade after first putting pen to paper, I am serenely grateful for each one of you that have stepped through the pages of this book with me. Thank you for the openness of your heart and the privilege of your time. Thank you for your willingness to be present, go deeper, and shift old stories to new possibilities. This is a luscious leadership that I am humbled by because I know that this is the kind of leadership that captivates and catalyzes new worlds.

As I look to the future, I am also serenely grateful for when I can say, "So, I met someone." I am mischievously restless to unwrap gifts I can't even imagine. And, I am delighted because I know the vast expanse of gloriously intimate possibilities that exist in the, "Now, What?"...that comes ever so tenderly after the, "So, I met someone."

My Invitation to You

$\mathcal{S}$imple, straightforward, to be used anytime: Gratitude Kick-starters. There's no wrong way to do this—you can write them down, you can do this walking, taking a shower, or driving to work. Simple action, huge returns!

- What three things am I grateful for about me / how I handled something today?
- What three things am I grateful for about my team / coworkers/boss?
- What three things am I grateful for about my relationship / my partner/mate?
- What three things am I grateful for about my home?
- What three things am I grateful for about my workspace?

I admire, applaud, and appreciate your courage,
XO, Danna

---

* *Do you desire space to reflect and journal? Visit the "Invitation to Go Deeper" section at the end of the book.*

Party Favors

Dear 'Gift of Men' Reader,

It takes great courage to have read this book, engaged with the content, and embraced a different possibility for men and women.

Thank you for being a VIP- a very inspiring person!

My special gift for you: receive the downloadable Gift of Men Journal, future updates on what the book is creating in the world, online book club and workshop information, and my weekly radio show reminder.

Please visit https://www.dannalewis.com/gift-of-men-vip to get the downloadable Gift of Men Journal.

xo, Danna

Afterparty:
More Possibilities

*D*ear 'Gift of Men' Reader,
   I would like to take this opportunity to invite you to discover both my Luscious Leadership Coaching Program and Gift of Men Coaching Program. The beauty that I have discovered within this book and throughout my life is the continued choice of personal leadership. As I engage with the energy of this type of consciousness I have been able to empower my best life. The result is the gift of elevating the world in a way that only I can. What gift and contribution can you be to yourself and uniquely to the world?

The Luscious Leadership Coaching Program is a 3-month one-on-one deeply guided program to become more deeply present, strategically aware, and courageously kind in the creation of whole-life wellbeing for yourself. You will learn tools to intercept burnout, manage high-sensitivity and empathic natures, declutter energetic and physical limitations, and implement pragmatic ways to consciously create the life you desire.

The Gift of Men Coaching Program is a 3-month one-on-one deeply guided program aligned with the exercises and invitations in the book. You will become more deeply present with what is true for you in love and relationships, clear limitations from past heartaches and beliefs, and begin to create the romantic life you truly desire.

To learn more about both programs, visit: https:// www.dannalewis.com

To stay in the loop about online book club and workshops, subscribe to the newsletter here: https://www.dannalewis.com/

To hire Danna to speak at an event, please contact Danna here: https://www.dannalewis.com/contact

Find Danna on LinkedIn: https://www.linkedin.com/in/dannalewispf/

Find Danna on Facebook: https://www.facebook.com/DannaLewisPublicFigure/

Find Danna on Instagram: https://www.instagram.com/danna_lewis_public_figure

Find Danna on Twitter: https://twitter.com/DannaLewisPF

About the Author

*D*ANNA LEWIS is a personal leadership coach, conscious business advisor, energy healer, and empath. She has more than 20 years of business experience in Director to COO level roles across multiple industries ranging from high-growth start-ups to Fortune 500 companies. Danna thoughtfully brings her education in quantum physics and consciousness to every aspect of her life, living, and business.

She has co-authored three Amazon best-selling books and hosts a weekly syndicated radio show/podcast, Luscious Leadership (find it on Inspired Choices Network, iHeart, Spotify, Stitcher, Apple, etc...)

Danna is known for working with highly sensitive and empathic people. She is also known for advocating for the power and pleasure that is available in romantic partnership and whole-life wellbeing as a vital foundation to more enjoyable, sustainable success. Her desire is for a world filled with people choosing to lead their lives with deeper presence, strategic awareness, and courageous kindness, ultimately contributing to the energetic shifts required for a thriving, sustainable planet.

By engaging the energy, each person can be empowered to their best life and elevate the world. Danna lives in San Francisco, CA and enjoys much of her time north of the city in Marin County.

Book Club
Reading Guide

- What was your initial response to the book?
- The author has a desire to invite the reader to be more present in their life and past experiences, did you sense that invitation?
- Was there a time while reading the book that you were able to discover the gift in a past situation, what was it?
- Through reading the book, and (possibly) engaging with the end of chapter invitations and exercises, do you feel more empowered?
- Through reading the book, and (possibly) engaging with the end of chapter invitations and exercises, do you have more gratitude for past relationships and lovers?
- Which chapter/story did you relate to the most, and what was it that connected with you?
- In what ways do you feel different after reading the book?

- Share a favorite quote or passage from the book and what impacted you about this quote or passage.
- What aspects of the author's story could you relate to most?
- Think about the other people in the book besides the author, how would you feel to have been depicted in this way?
- If you got the chance to ask the author one question, what would it be?

Just for fun...
- Do you think this book would make a good movie or TV series?
- If the book were being adapted into a movie/TV series, who would you want to see play what parts?
- What would you like to see/not see if it was turned into a movie/TV series?

An Invitation to Go Deeper: Reflection and Journal Space

*D*id you like the invitations at the end of each chapter to reflect and transform aspects and experiences but desire some writing space? Here it is! Here is your special space to journal and align your actions.

> *I admire, applaud, and appreciate your courage,*
> *XO, Danna*

From Chapter 1
The Invitation

If you could get anything out of reading this book and the 'Going Deeper' section, what would it be?

From Chapter 2
The RSVP: The Gift of Presence

I invite you to reflect on the present.

Things don't always show up the way you think they will; that invite to your nephew's baseball game may lead you right to your lifelong partner or new best friend or business opportunity. Be willing to check in with yourself and trust the whisper of awareness that is lighting your path to the something greater that you have been asking for.

What invitations, perhaps to something you've been asking for, literal and otherwise have you perhaps missed or ignored?

From Chapter 3
The Empty Box: The Gift of Possibility

Grab a cup of tea or cocoa or perhaps a glass of wine or a cocktail, turn off your phone. I promise the sky won't fall and whoever or whatever is needing you will survive the next few minutes without your instant reply ... really, it's all about you right now!

Take a deep breath and with Harrison-Ford-Indiana-Jones curiosity and courage, go back into the empty box of one of your dark nights. Stand in the middle of that total darkness, knowing you are safe and sound in the present. Stand in the middle of that total darkness and be still with it. Stand in the middle of that empty box that you had and ask yourself this: If I could suspend my belief that anything here was right or wrong; that I must defend for or against my story, the story, could there be a new possibility to light the way?

Barriers down, vulnerability up, was there an unacknowledged spiritual healing occurring? Beyond the surface decisions, thoughts, and meanings of a dark time, could it have actually been a spiritual healing experience that was required to restore harmony to your being? A deep learning created to consciously reconnect with your inner truth and wisdom?

Allow yourself to notice the clues lingering in the corners, longing for your attention. Was your dark night actually moments of change and transformation threaded together by your demand for something greater to show up in your life? Were the actions of purging, of drastic change, of intense pain and hurt the clearing of what was no longer serving you?

Use this space to journal about a spiritual healing experience.

From Chapter 4

Transportation: The Gift of Perception and Wisdom

Who's ready for a turning point in the road to the super-highway of consciousness? Just for you, I have a few fun tools to jumpstart you in shifting the gears on your perspective. Start asking the following questions when looking for the gift:

1. What's right about this I'm not getting?
2. What point of view would I have to shift, change, or give up for this to turn out greater than I can imagine?
3. When all else fails: "Universe, show me the gift here."

And, please, please, please invoke your sometimes-impossible patience and do not rush, push, or plot for an answer. Discovering the gift is an unfolding, a soft whisper of awareness, a gentle release, and yes, sometimes a thunderous roar. Hmmm, like our sometimes-elusive orgasms ladies, the awareness of the gift cannot be forced, it will come when it chooses to come!

What is an experience with a lover (past or present) that when you use these tools to shift the perception, the gift becomes more clear?

From Chapter 5
Shopping: The Gift of Intention and Choice

It's list time! It may be very tempting to do this with a group of friends, so let me hazard you with this question: will their thoughts and points of view affect or color yours? Will you have the space to be super vulnerable with yourself, allowing something that is uniquely true for you to come through? Clear, honest communication with yourself is the key here. Conversation, comparison, and collaboration with the ladies are not. Now is the time to get clear and state what YOU desire — whether it be a boyfriend, a spouse, a lover (or two) or a lifelong partner. It's also the space to identify dealbreakers, whether it's no drugs, no small children, no crazy exes or something else, get real with what you're okay and not okay with. It's your life, and these things impact your daily experience. Please also include the extra juicy things you desire to contribute to your person and vice versa.

No one, really, truly, no one else is going to do this for you or be the guardian and advocate for this dream the way you can. Let's begin.

I desire a:

I require from them:

My dealbreakers are:

My extra-juicy desires to contribute to them and receive from them are:

From Chapter 6

Wrapped in Cargo Shorts and a Hawaiian Shirt: The Gift of Self, Freedom, and Forgiveness

*G*etting jiggy with it! We (me, the mouse in my pocket, and any of you that are willing) are going to do a forgiveness and freedom exercise with all the men we've dated. Really. No, really. Jot them all down. If they pop into your head, write their name down!

Now, without having to walk down the minute and mind-numbing details of memory lane with each guy, ask yourself these questions for each name, and in asking the question, let's work on trusting our awareness and our gut, especially if you notice a pull, a tug, a hurt in your Universe.

Before you begin, identify or journal about the person(s) you are bringing into the forgiveness exercise:

- Truth, is there something here that I believe I need to forgive this man for?
    - No? Great, namaste, next question.
    - Yes? Then here are some more questions to play with to open the space: Is it still relevant? Can I acknowledge it's no longer relevant and let it go? (Big deep breath) Was there an expectation that he act, behave, or respond the way you or a girlfriend would? (Men are men, not women, and we so often set ourselves up when we expect them to respond like women do.) Is it possible, he was doing the best he could, given the circumstances, his experiences, and the tools he had at the time? How has holding on to this affected my life? And, if I continue to hold on to it, will it decay or contribute to my life? Am I willing to let this go and allow the energies that have been locked up by this to loiter in my life and live in a sparkly, new way?
- Truth, is there something here that I believe I need to forgive myself for?
    - No? Great, namaste, next question.

• Yes? Here are some more questions to play with to open the space: Is it still relevant? Can I acknowledge it's no longer relevant and let it go? (Big, deep breath.) Or was I possibly doing the best I could, given the circumstances, my experiences, and the tools I had at the time? How has holding on to this affected my life? And, if I continue to hold on to it, will it decay or contribute to my life? What would I tell my best friend if this was her and she was holding a grudge or grievance with herself? Am I willing to let this go and allow the energies that have been locked up by this to loiter in my life and live in a sparkly, new way?

Please take a few moments to journal about the shifts you've experienced through this exercise. What are you aware of?

Journal page.

From Chapter 7

Wrapped in a Black Cashmere Sports Coat and a Glass of Wine: The Gift of Excitement, Encouragement, and Harmony

*F*rom deal-breaking remorse to deal-breaking delight, let's shift some sh*t. Remember that list we worked on and created in Chapter 5? And, remember the forgiveness exercises we did in Chapter 6? Well, we are going to put them together like a celebrity couple mash-up.

If you're like me, you're an experiential learner with a zest for pleasure-seeking adventures. So, what if you're not wrong for choosing a dealbreaker situation? What if you're never wrong for being you, living life, and "learning" forward? This man, this chapter in my life, while clearly having one of my dealbreakers, also very clearly dealt me a winning hand in experiences that will continue to nurture my desires long into the future. Take those learning hands, hold them close to the chest, and let them nurture your desires long into your future love(s).

This is super simple: journal about a love experience that you chose that was in opposition to a known dealbreaker of yours. And then let it go. Forgive yourself, if needed (see forgiveness exercise.) Please give yourself permission to move forward, if you haven't already.

Journal page.

From Chapter 8

Wrapped in a Tie-Dyed Tee Shirt and a Minivan: The Gift of Passion, Music, and Healing

It's a beautiful thing to acknowledge the serendipity of the Universe bringing people into our lives to expand it, heal it, and ignite it. It's a very beautifully empowering thing to ignite our own flames. This exercise helps us fan our own flames and feed our own joy and desires. And we can utilize our men, what we've received from them, as the kindling.

In the center of the following page, write down one of your guy's names. Now, form spokes out

from his name with the gifts you received from him (music, excitement, freedom, etc...) Then create arrows (the 'sparks') from each gift and identify at least one activity or thing you can do or add to your life that creates that same effect/feeling for you. You'll end up with a bonfire of possibilities for fueling your life.

From Chapter 9

Wrapped in Sneakers and a Cup of Tea: The Gift of Clarity, Adventure, and Friendship Chapter

In your adventure of living, what are your top five priorities? Come on, you knew that was coming! And, truly, what I know for sure is that by knowing these and reconfirming them every so often, everything in my life has become easier. Why? Because I can easily say yes to things that nurture my priorities and no to things that don't or at least be very aware of my choices.

My Top Five Priorities are:

1.

2.

3.

4.

5.

From Chapter 10

Wrapped in a Flannel Shirt and a Guitar: The Gift of Romance, Honesty, and Inspiration

*B*eyond the List. Here's the thing: having your list and knowing your priorities are incredibly valuable. Trusting your body's awareness is priceless. For the times someone has checked all the boxes on your list but you or they weren't attracted to your body and one of you ended things, be grateful, be very grateful. We're talking about romantic dating and partnership here, and if a long-term or lifelong partnership is something you seek, please add this to your list: there must be a mutual admiration and appreciation of each other as well as mutual affection, attraction, and adoring of each other's bodies.

I'm not talking about mind-blowing, can't breathe without him attraction; that has its own pitfalls. I'm talking about innate affection, caring, and yummy attraction to his home (his body). Meeting someone and expecting them to change or that you'll grow into liking their bodies more is not a kindness to them or you. Everyone deserves to be appreciated, admired, and adored by their lover – spouse for exactly who they are. And not having that oftentimes creates a disparate and disintegrating romantic partnership reduced to feeling like trapped roommates. The yum is possible; let your body give you information.

Take a few moment to reflect and journal on the where this has shown up for you in your relationships.

Journal page.

From Chapter 11

Regifting: The Gift of Contribution Chapter

Start an "acknowledgment of you" list! As I sift through my days, I jot down different choices and actions that are generating and engaging me in authentic ways. Some of my current acknowledgments include finding a book cover designer; submitting a proposal to speak at a women's organization; reaching out to someone I know through social media to meet for coffee; walking to the farmers' market for groceries; deleting a dating app that isn't feeling good; saying yes to the man I met in the grocery store. You get the idea. There are no rules except to not judge yourself for what you did or didn't do.

Start an "acknowledgment of him" list as well! Living intentionally includes acknowledging the energies and actions your guy is choosing that also feed your desires. He spent ten extra minutes in bed snuggling with you. He called your mom with you and chatted. He walked to the farmers' market with you and you shopped together. You get the idea. There are no rules except to not judge him for what he did or didn't do.

Acknowledgement List

-
-
-
-
-

From Chapter 12

Dessert: The Gift of 'Big Love' AKA Choice, Awareness, and Possibilities Chapter

How many of you only go into the bakery to look, refusing to indulge and enjoy what your heart desires? How many of you will only eat gluten-free bread or no bread at all when your body is screaming for that carrot cake? I challenge you to look at some of the rules you have chosen, and play with what your choices create when you choose from them and when you choose from joy, from what lights you up. Notice. Just notice. And, please, oh please, a tiny bit more, choose what you cherish and covet and enjoy the f@ck out of the possibilities those choices create.

Journal (or list) about what you covet, what you truly desire:

From Chapter 13

Afterglow

Let's Change the conversation! I was recently on a walk at Chrissy Field along the beach and while talking with a group of women, all in their 50s and 60s I had just met, this transpired: One of the women was telling the story about a harbor seal she had seen floating in the water with his flipper outstretched, waiting for the nearby fishermen on the pier to throw him bait to eat. Another of the women remarked, "He's a lazy one, just like all men." Whoa! I was floored, how do you go from telling a cute story about a harbor seal to lambasting all men in one fell swoop?! I was speechless and, for several reasons, did not respond. One, I had just met these people, and I suppose I didn't want to confront or affront anyone. And two, I'm not very quick on my feet and couldn't think of anything to say in a gracious, succinct, and inviting (of another possibility) way. Let's just say this was on my mind, and in my heart, so much that I did come up with some things I could have said.

SO, ladies, what if we use our strength, vulnerability, and power to change the conversation and perhaps say this, not that...

- "All men are lazy."
  - Oh gosh, I'm sorry you've had that experience with *All* men. I know so many hard-working, industrious, creative, (fill in the blank) men.
- "Men are idiots and can't do anything right."
  - I know so many brilliant and smart men. I admire their thinking and have come to realize more and more that just because they do something maybe totally different than I would, it's just different, not wrong. And my way isn't necessarily right, just different. I'm really learning to appreciate how our brains may just be different!
- "I don't need a man or any men."
  - That's such an interesting comment to me. For me, personally, with the leadership work I've been doing, I have found that the more I'm open to receiving from everyone, men and women, the more gratitude I have, the greater my life becomes, and the more enjoyable everyone is.
- "Men are scum, dicks, assholes, etc."
  - Can we take that down a level? We all know how horrible it feels and incorrect it is when we are grouped and lumped together as

collective (unkind/untrue) generalizations. What else is possible?

Your turn. Journal or list some conversations/ comments that you can now shift into a 'Say This, Not That'

From Chapter 14

The Thank You Note: The Gift of Gratitude

Simple, straightforward, to be used anytime: Gratitude Kick-starters. There's no wrong way to do this. Simple action, huge returns!

#GratitudeGrowsGreatness

What are three things I am grateful for about me?
1.

2.

3.

What are three things I am grateful for about my spouse?
1.

2.

3.

What are three things I am grateful for about my relationship?

1.

2.

3.

What are three things I am grateful for about my home?

1.

2.

3.

What are three things I am grateful for about my coworkers?

1.

2.

3.

What are three things I am grateful for about my workspace?

1.

2.

3.

Thank you for going deeper throughout these journal pages.
XO, Danna

A Reminder: Party Favors

Dear 'Gift of Men' Reader,

It takes great courage to have read this book, engaged with the content, and embraced a different possibility for men and women.

Thank you for being a VIP- a very inspiring person!

My special gift for you: receive the downloadable Gift of Men Journal, future updates on what the book is creating in the world, online book club and workshop information, and my weekly radio show reminder.

Please visit https://www.dannalewis.com/gift-of-men-vip to get the downloadable Gift of Men Journal.

xo, Danna

Made in the USA
San Bernardino, CA
09 December 2019

61160142R00146